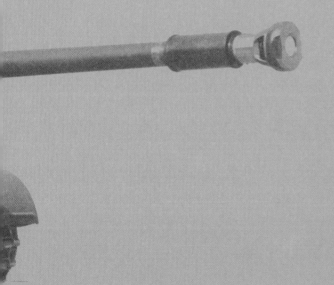

LEGENDS OF WARFARE

GROUND

M26 Pershing

America's Medium/Heavy Tank in World War II and Korea

DAVID DOYLE

SCHIFFER MILITARY

4880 Lower Valley Road ■ Atglen, PA 19310

Designed by Justin Watkinson
Type set in Impact/Minion Pro/Univers LT Std

ISBN: 978-0-7643-6640-6
Printed in India

Published by Schiffer Publishing, Ltd.
4880 Lower Valley Road
Atglen, PA 19310
Phone: (610) 593 1777; Fax: (610) 593 2002
Email: Info@schifferbooks.com
Web: www.schifferbooks.com

For our complete selection of fine books on this and related subjects, please visit our website at www.schifferbooks.com. You may also write for a free catalog.

Schiffer Publishing's titles are available at special discounts for bulk purchases for sales promotions or premiums. Special editions, including personalized covers, corporate imprints, and excerpts, can be created in large quantities for special needs. For more information, contact the publisher.

We are always looking for people to write books on new and related subjects. If you have an idea for a book, please contact us at proposals@schifferbooks.com.

Acknowledgments

This book would not have been possible without the gracious help of many individuals and institutions. Beyond the invaluable help provided by the staffs of Fiat-Chrysler North America, General Motors, the TACOM LCMC History Office, the National Archives, and the Patton Museum, I am deeply indebted to Tom Kailbourn, Scott Taylor, the late Richard Hunnicutt, Dana Bell, Chun Hsu, and Joe DeMarco. Their generous and skillful assistance adds immensely to the quality of this volume. In addition to such wonderful friends and colleagues, the Lord has blessed me with a wonderful wife, Denise, who has tirelessly scanned thousands of photos and documents for this and numerous other books. Beyond that, she is an ongoing source of support and inspiration.

Contents

Introduction

By early 1942, American Sherman tanks were shown to be outgunned, and lacking in armor, compared to their German adversaries. Further, the infantry branch desired a tank with heavier armor, even if slower than the Sherman, to support infantry operations. This desire led to a succession of experimental vehicles: the T14, T20, T22, and T23, and various derivatives thereof. Some of these tanks also incorporated torsion-bar suspension rather the volute spring suspension commonly used in US tanks to that point. Also the drivetrain was rearranged, such that the tracks were driven at the rear of the tank, rather than the front. The prior design of front drive meant that a driveshaft had to extend under or through the fighting compartment to the front of the vehicle. This required a much-higher profile in order to provide the needed clearance beneath the turret. The T23 was notable in that it introduced the concept of gas-electric tank drive in the US Army.

As the T23E3 pilot was being created, US forces in the Kasserine Pass encountered the German Tiger. This experience caused the armored force to revisit its criteria for tank design, wanting both a more powerful gun and heavier armor than afforded by the Sherman, moving their desires to be more closely aligned with infantry's.

In May 1943, development of two new tank designs began in response to the Armored Forces post-Kasserine opinion. These were the T25 and T26 tanks. The two designs were to be similar, with the T26 having heavier armor. Both the T25 and T26 were to use gas-electric drive, with a Ford GAN gasoline engine running a generator, which supplied current that would drive electric motors to propel the tank. The tanks used horizontal-volute suspension. By the time the T25 reached pilot stage, its weight had reached 81,000 pounds, and the T26 was expected to weigh about 4 tons more. In both cases, a considerable portion of the weight was attributable to the gas-electric drive.

Because of this, modified designs—designated T25E1 and T26E1—were created. The new designs replaced the gas-electric drivetrain with a more conventional drivetrain with a Ford GAF V-8 gasoline engine and Torqmatic transmission. Fifty of these vehicles, forty T25E1s and ten T26E1s, were ordered for trial, and deliveries began in February 1944. All were built at the Fisher Grand Blanc tank arsenal and were armed with the 90 mm T7 gun. The first two T26E1s were shipped to Aberdeen Proving Ground in Maryland in February.

As fall 1943 arrived, time was becoming critical if US forces were to have a new, improved tank to invade Europe with. Lt. Gen. Jacob Devers, who at the time was commander of US forces in Europe and was the former chief of the Armored Force, requested development be accelerated and that 250 T26E1s be procured as quickly as possible, to which Ordnance agreed. However, the request had to be approved by the Army Ground Forces first. The head of Army Ground Forces (AGF) at the time was Lt. Gen. Leslie McNair, who strongly disapproved, stating, "The M4 tank, particularly the M4A3, has been widely hailed as the best tank on the battlefield today. There are indications that the enemy concurs in this view. Apparently, the M4 is an ideal combination of mobility, dependability, speed, protection and firepower. Other than this particular request—which represents the British view—there has been no call from any theater for a 90 mm tank gun." He continued, essentially reciting US policy of the time concerning tank destroyers, "There can be no basis for the T26 tank other than from the conception of tank versus tank duel—which is believed unsound and unnecessary. Both British and American battle experience has demonstrated that the antitank gun in suitable numbers and dispersed properly is the master of the tank."

The T20 medium tank, development of which began in the spring of 1942 as an eventual replacement for the M4 medium tank, represented a US effort to keep apace with recent improvements in German armor, especially with respect to protection and firepower. The first pilot T20 was completed in May 1943 and featured a rear-mounted transmission, a 500-horsepower Ford GAN V8 gasoline engine, and a horizontal-volute suspension system. The maximum armor thickness was 3.5 inches on the turret and 2.5 inches on the glacis, which was set at 47 degrees from vertical; in these areas, the M4A3 medium tank had the same specifications. The transmission was the Detroit Transmission Torqmatic, a torque-converter, fluid-drive model. The T20E3, depicted here, was similar to the T20 but with a torsion-bar suspension. The main armament was the M1A1 76 mm gun on the T79 mount. *TACOM LCMC History Office*

Model	M26	M26A1	M45
Weight*	92,000	92,000	92,500
Length**	333.625	333.625	252
Width**	137	137	138
Height**	109	109	109
Track	110	110	110
Track width	24" (T81)	24" (T81)	23" (T80E1 & T84E1)
Crew	5	5	5
Maximum speed, mph	30	30	30
Fuel capacity, gal.	191	191	191
Range, miles	92	92	100
Electrical	24 negative	24 negative	24 negative
Torqmatic transmission speeds	3	3	3
Turning radius, feet	31	31	31
Armament			
Main	90 mm	90 mm	105 mm
Secondary	2 × .30 cal.	2 × .30 cal.	2 × .30 cal.
Flexible	1 × .50 cal.	1 × .50 cal.	1 × .50 cal.

Engine Data	
Engine make/model	Ford GAF
Number of cylinders	60-degree V-8
Cubic-inch displacement	1,000
Horsepower	500 @ 2,600
Torque	950 @ 2,100
Governed speed (rpm)	2,600

Radio Equipment

A variety of radio equipment was mounted in this family of tanks, including SCR-508, SCR-608, or SCR-528, all with interphone set RC298, or AN/VRC-3 and RC-99 interphone set.

* Fighting weight, lbs.
** Overall dimensions listed in inches

In early 1943, the first pilot T23 medium tank was completed. Like the T20, it was equipped with a Ford GAN engine and a vertical-volute suspension system, akin to that of the M4 medium tanks, but it had an electric-drive transmission, which proved faulty during testing. The main armament for the pilots remained the M1A1 76 mm gun on the T79 mount. The bow machine gun had a boxy enclosure. This is the second pilot T23, registration number W-3098788, on August 29, 1944. A total of 250 production T23s were completed. *TACOM LCMC History Office*

One pilot T23E3 medium tank was built, by Chrysler: registration number 30103068. It is shown at the factory on July 24, 1944. It was similar to the M23 medium tank but was equipped with torsion-bar suspension. The vehicle did not go into series production, owing to problems with the electric-drive transmission. However, the turret and 76 mm gun, also used on T23s, proved to be very effective and was produced for M4A1, M4A2, and M4A3 medium tanks. *FCA North America Archives*

Chrysler converted two pilot T25 medium tanks from T23 medium tanks. They were powered by Ford GAN engines through electric-drive transmissions and were fitted with horizontal-volute spring suspensions and 23-inch center-guided tracks. Chrysler delivered the first pilot in January 1944. The main armament was the T7 90 mm gun (standardized as M3) on a T99 mount. The hump on the top of the glacis was to accommodate a ventilator. The commander had a rotating cupola with vision blocks on the right side of the turret roof, while the loader had a rotating cupola with split doors and a socket for an antiaircraft machine-gun mount. *FCA North America Archives*

Based on Allied lessons learned from combat with the German Tiger I tank, the US Army ordered that forty T23s be converted to T25E1 medium tanks. These were equipped with Torqmatic transmissions, torsion-bar suspensions with dual bogie wheels, and the M3 90 mm gun in a T99 Mount. Armor protection of the T25E1 was lighter than on the concurrently developed T26E1, and hence its combat-loaded weight, 77,590 pounds, was almost 5 tons less than the combat-loaded weight of the T26E1, 87,350 pounds. *US Army Armor & Cavalry Collection*

The Tank Laboratory of the Chrysler Engineering Division produced a single pilot T26 heavy tank, registration number 30128307, delivering it on October 28, 1944. It featured torsion-bar suspension with dual bogie wheels, 24-inch tracks, electric-drive transmission and Ford GAN engine, and the same type of turret used on the T26E1, with a T7 (M3) 90 mm gun in a T99E1 mount. *FCA North America Archives*

As seen in a photo of the pilot T26 at the Chrysler Engineering Division plant on October 21, 1944, a pistol port was included on the left side of the turret, on a flat plate welded to the turret casting. The tracks were the type T81, a single-pin design with openings near the outer sides of each shoe for engaging the sprocket teeth. Stiffeners were stamped into the mudguards and sand shields. Above the loader's hatch is a .50-caliber machine gun with a dustcover; on the rear of the turret bustle are brackets for storing the machine gun during travel. *FCA North America Archives*

General Motors Fisher Tank Arsenal, Grand Blanc, Michigan, manufactured ten T26E1 medium tanks. Like the T25E1, this tank was powered by a Ford GAF engine and Torqmatic transmission and had a torsion-bar suspension, but the T26E1 had heavier armor than the T25E1. In this view of the first T26E1, on the right side of the turret is a rack for storing two foul-weather hoods, for the driver's and assistant driver's hatches. The aperture for the gunner's telescopic sight is sunken into the right side of the gun shield, or mantlet. The main armament was the same as on the T26: the T7 (M3) 90 mm gun in a T99E1 mount. A .50-caliber M2 HB machine gun is on the mount on the loader's cupola, its barrel secured in the travel lock. *US Army Armor & Cavalry Collection*

The Pershing tanks were noticeably larger than the Shermans in height, width, length, and weight. This comparative photo illustrates that fact, although the Sherman actually appears slightly smaller, with reference to the Pershing, than its actual dimensions would indicate. A close view of the image reveals a registration number on the ventilator bulge at the top of the glacis of the Pershing; the first two numbers are lost in the glare, but the remainder is 120059, so this T26E3 would appear to be registration number 30120059, or serial number 249. *US Army Armor & Cavalry Collection*

CHAPTER 1
T26E3 Enters Production

Having been rebuffed by both McNair and Eisenhower (and later Patton), Devers took his case directly to the War Department. On December 16, 1943, the War Department authorized the production of 250 of the vehicles, with slight refinements, which were designated T26E3. These were beyond the ten pilot tanks already authorized. Even with this, the new tank continued to meet opposition, including from Gen. George Patton, who advocated the retention of the M4, armed with 75 mm gun. The new tank did find a champion in Brig. Gen. Maurice Rose, however. McNair continued to dabble in the program, recommending that the light T25E1 be produced rather than the T26E3, and that the armament be changed to 76 mm rather than 90 mm. Fortunately, he did not sway the War Department, which eschewed his recommendation in favor of increasing the order to two thousand tanks, 10 percent of which were to be armed with a 105 mm howitzer rather than 90 mm cannon. The howitzer-armed tanks were designated T26E2. In time, the two-thousand-tank order would be increased to six thousand tanks.

On June 29, 1944, the designation of the vehicle was officially changed to heavy tank.

At last, in November 1944, production of the T26E3 began at the Fisher Tank Arsenal, ramping up rapidly. In March, this was augmented by additional production at the Chrysler-operated Detroit Tank Arsenal.

Events following the Normandy invasion had confirmed that both the German Panther and Tiger were superior to the US Sherman, but the extensive training of the US tankers, as well as the mechanical reliability and abundance of the Sherman, allowed them to overcome their armor and armament disadvantages.

However, the Germans' Ardennes Offensive in December 1944 sent the US forces reeling. American tank losses were reaching alarming levels. Maj. Gen. Gladeon Barnes, chief of research and engineering for the Ordnance Department, wanted to send half of the T26E3s existing at the end of 1944 to Europe. Army Ground Forces strongly opposed this, in part due to logistics, but relented when Barnes vowed to the Army chief of staff, Gen. George Marshall, to get T26E3s into the field in Europe. Dubbed the Zebra Mission, the twenty T26E3s, along with other experimental weapons such as the T83, were sent to Antwerp, arriving in January 1945.

Testing of the ten T26E1s disclosed some weaknesses, including mechanical problems and insufficient storage space for main-armament ammunition. When the Army submitted an order for an additional 250 T26E1s, improvements from the tests were incorporated into the new vehicles, and they were redesignated as the T26E3 heavy tank (after the war, they would be redesignated as medium tanks). Production of the T26E3s commenced at the Fisher Tank Arsenal in November 1944. Serial numbers of these vehicles began at 11. This vehicle is the second T26E3, serial number 12, seen during tests at Aberdeen Proving Ground, Maryland, on December 22, 1944. These vehicles retained the rack for the drivers' foul-weather hoods on the right side of the turret. *US Army Armor & Cavalry Collection*

The same T26E3 is viewed from the left side at Aberdeen. A round pistol port with a hinge on the rear side was on the left side of the turret. Spare track shoes were stowed on this side of the turret, one vertically and three horizontally; to the rear of them, stored vertically, is a track-connecting and link-pulling fixture, also called a track jack, used in repairing and replacing tracks. The two similar fittings located to the front of the bottom of the forward-stored track shoe, and to the rear of the bottom of the track jack, were brackets for attaching a hoist for removing and installing the power pack (the engine and transmission). This feature also was present on the T25E1 and T26E1. A muzzle brake now was fitted on the 90 mm gun, to reduce the amount of dust kicked up when the gun was fired. *US Army Armor & Cavalry Collection*

The turret of T26E3, serial number 12, is traversed to the rear, in travel position, with the front of the barrel seated in the rest on the rear of the engine deck. Since an oval hatch had replaced the loader's cupola, it was necessary to install a new, pedestal machine-gun mount on the top of the turret bustle. Here, an unusual twin .50-caliber M2 HB machine-gun combination has been mounted on the pedestal. *US Army Armor & Cavalry Collection*

The bow of the T26 comprised a single casting, incorporating the glacis, the section below the glacis, and the top of the drivers' compartment. Two pairs of towing eyes are welded to the lower part of the glacis. The registration number of this example, undergoing testing in the winter, is legible on the bulge for the ventilator at the top of the glacis, although the last two digits are indistinct: it appears to be 30119898. Above the sand shields are storage boxes for vehicular and crew equipment. *US Army Armor & Cavalry Collection*

Workers at the Fisher Tank Arsenal are feeding a torsion bar into the top of a suspension arm. The torsion bars acted in lieu of springs, with one end connected to the top of the arm and the other to the opposite side of the hull. Other arms are mounted, as well as five dual track-support rollers, sprocket (rear), shock absorbers for the first and second bogies (shock absorbers also were provided for the last two bogies), and, to the front of the first shock absorber, a bump-spring assembly. Jutting from the upper hull are beams, which will support the fender. *General Motors LLC*

As seen from the right rear of a T26E3 chassis under construction at the Fisher Tank Arsenal, the sprocket is in the foreground, track-support rollers are below the level of the fender supports, and below are the bogie arms, shock absorbers, bump springs, and bogie-wheel hubs. In the background, a mechanic is installing an inner bogie wheel. *US Army Armor & Cavalry Collection*

Turrets for T26E3s are under assembly. On the closest one, the white interior of the turret is visible through the opening for the gun. The loader's hatch and separate periscope with brush guard are installed. The commander's cupola and, to the front of it, the gunner's periscope have yet to be installed. The 90 mm guns and mounts, including the shields, have been installed on the other turrets. L-shaped vane sights are mounted on the turret roofs to the fronts of the commander's cupolas on at least the second and third turrets, and fixtures in the form of steel rods have been installed on the fronts of the turrets and on the sides and tops of the gun shields for attaching dustcovers. The front ends of the 90 mm gun tubes are threaded, to accept muzzle brakes. *General Motors LLC*

Workers at the Fisher Tank Arsenal are lowering a turret onto a T26E3 chassis. These turrets lacked a turret basket. On the far side of the turret are the two curved arms that supported the gunner's seat; on the bottom front of the turret is the traversing motor. On the side of the turret is a clear view of the brackets for storing spare track shoes. On the upper part of the gun shield is the casting mark, "E10609." Tape is over the port for the coaxial machine gun. *General Motors LLC*

At least nineteen T26E3s and, in the background, a similar number of large-hatch HVSS Shermans are under assembly at the Fisher Tank Arsenal. Turrets for the T26E3s are on stands on the left side of the photo, with dustcovers installed between the gun shields and the fronts of the turrets. Guards made of sticks bound together with wire are over the muzzle brakes, which also have dustcovers over them. Retainer straps are on the tops of the storage racks for the drivers' foul-weather hoods. The pedestal mounts for the antiaircraft machine guns on the turret roofs had hinges on the rears of the bases, to allow them to be lowered and secured with straps during travel. *US Army Armor & Cavalry Collection*

Mudguards have been installed on these T26E3s under assembly. These vehicles as well as the Pershings in the two preceding photos were equipped with a RotoClone blower, rated at 400 cubic feet per minute (cfm), in the upper center of the drivers' compartment. A slight bulge on the top center of the glacis provided clearance for the blower. Tests proved that this blower was not up to the task of evacuating propellant fumes from the vehicle when the guns were being fired. Thus a larger, 1,000 cfm blower was installed. *US Army Armor & Cavalry Collection*

The enlarged bulge on the top of the glacis that accompanied the installation of the 1,000 cfm blower in the T26E3 is present on this vehicle being assembled at Fisher. The 1,000 cfm blowers were introduced with tank number 550 at Fisher and 235 at Chrysler. Hulls with this blower lacked the two drivers' periscopes mounted between the hatch doors and the blower. This is the final Fisher T26E3, serial number 1739, which is chalked on the glacis along with the notation "LAST ONE." This tank was completed in October 1945. *Sloan Museum*

Fisher Tank Arsenal executives and workers are posing with what appears to be the final T26E3 to be completed, in October 1945. With the end of T26E3 production at Fisher, the arsenal had completed 1,729 vehicles. T80E1 tracks, with chevron grousers and two pins, are installed. *Grand Blanc Heritage Museum*

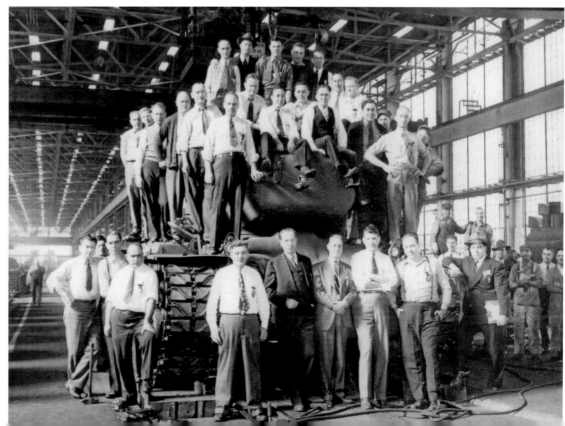

Beginning in March 1945, Chrysler began producing T26E3s at the Detroit Tank Arsenal, in Warren, Michigan, completing 473 units before that plant ceased work on that model in August 1945. Although the placard in the foreground states that this is the "No. 1 Heavy Tank T-26, E3-90mm," the registration number, faintly visible on the ventilator bulge at the top of the glacis, is 30128311, which was actually the fifth Chrysler T26E3, serial number 30128307 being the first one. The crate to the front of the tank contained spare parts and accessories. *US Army Armor & Cavalry Collection*

A rear view of the same T26E3 shows details on the rear of the tank, including the tow pintle stored to the upper left of the pintle's bracket, and the travel lock, which was mounted with bolts to the exhaust. The muzzle brake and the joint between the 90 mm gun tube and the gun shield have been sealed to keep out moisture during shipping. *US Army Armor & Cavalry Collection*

T26E3 registration number 30128311 has been secured to the flatcar and is ready for shipment, on March 21, 1945. This was about a month after Fisher-produced T26E3s had begun active operations in Germany. Behind the fence in the left background are Sherman tanks. *US Army Armor & Cavalry Collection*

Chassis of T26E3 heavy tanks are under assembly at the Detroit Tank Factory, with an example with the turret installed parked to the left. These are early-to-middle-production vehicles, with the 400 cfm ventilation blowers and periscopes inboard of the drivers' hatches. T80E1 double-pin tracks are installed. Among the parts stored to the right of the tank with the turret are escape hatches for the drivers' compartment, and rolls of fabric, possibly dustcovers for the gun shields. *FCA North America Archives*

Detroit Arsenal workers are guiding a turret down onto a T26E3 chassis. The dustcover on this turret was a type that completely enclosed the gun shield, with the front of the cover secured to the gun tube with a ring. *US Army Armor & Cavalry Collection*

T26E3s in various states of completion are assembled in an area of the Detroit Tank Arsenal. As seen on the closest tank, the dustcover that enclosed the entire gun shield had round openings for the coaxial machine gun and the gunner's telescopic sight. A feature not present on the earliest T26E3s was the brace from the rear of each fender to the hull, with a turnbuckle in the center for adjusting the tension. *FCA North America Archives*

A recently completed T26E3 with a 1,000 cfm blower has paused outside the Detroit Tank Arsenal, with a sign proclaiming the receipt of an Army-Navy "E" for excellence award on the building. Instead of rods welded on the turret to the sides of and above the gun shield, for attaching a dustcover, this vehicle has small, square bosses, tapped to accept screws. This feature is visible on some of the preceding factory photos of Chrysler T26E3s. Sections of rods, bent at a 90-degree angle, were welded on the turret where the upper corners of the dustcover was attached to the turret. *FCA North America Archives*

A new T26E3 is being lowered toward a flatcar in the Detroit Tank Arsenal. Taillight assemblies and guards are on the sides of the rear of the hull. Near the rear of the left fender is an armored box for a first-aid kit. The top of the registration number is faintly visible on the side of the rear storage container, to the front of the first-aid kit, but is not legible. *FCA North America Archives*

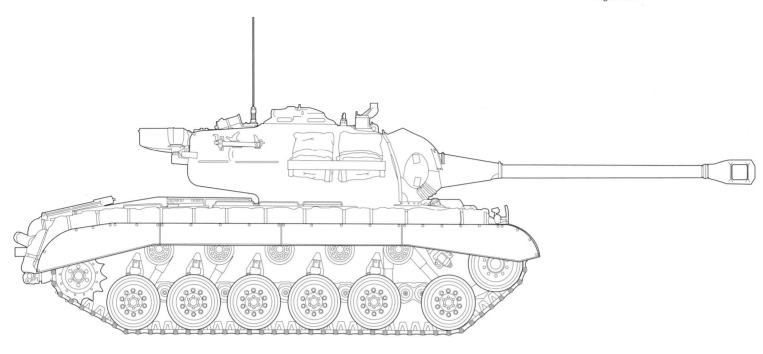

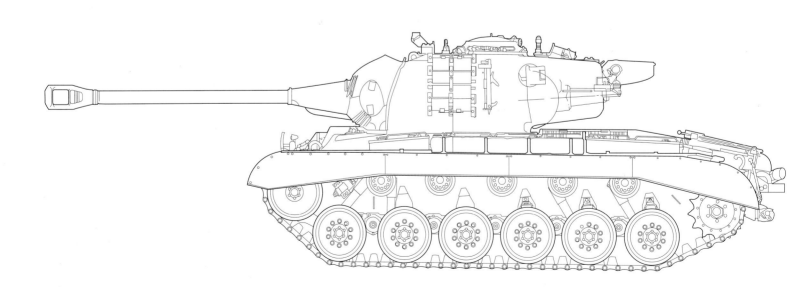

Interior

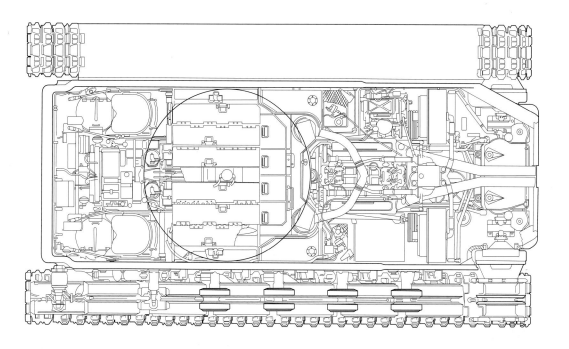

Top

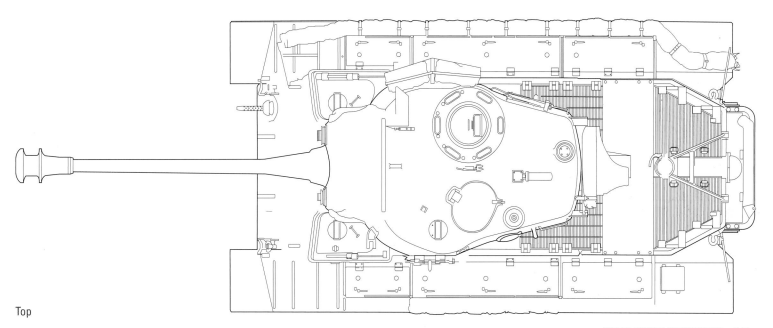

The new T26E3s were assigned to Omar Bradley's 12th Army Group, 1st Army. Half were assigned to the 3rd Armored Division, with the balance being assigned to the 9th Armored Division. The tanks had been accompanied by experts, including Captain Elmer Gray, and Slim Price, a civilian 90 mm gun expert from Aberdeen.

On February 25, 1945, the T26E3 entered combat for the first time, with Task Force Lovelady fighting for the Roer River. The next night they suffered their first casualty when a T26E3 was ambushed, presumably by a Tiger I of Pz.Abt.(Fkl.) 301. Sadly, two American tankers were killed, but the T26E3 was repaired and returned to combat in a few days.

On February 27 a T26E3 from Company E, 33rd Armored Regiment, got revenge, knocking out a Tiger I as well as two Panzer IVs near Elsdorf. The Tiger was taken at 900 yards, and the Panzer IVs at 1,200 yards, a range well beyond the previous maximum for US tanks.

In more action near the Roer in February, another T26E3 was disabled when struck twice by a German 150 mm gun. With four tanks left in Lt. John Grimball's heavy-tank platoon of the 14th Tank Battalion, the unit would make history. On March 7, 1945, armored infantry of Combat Command B, 9th Armored Division, discovered that the imposing Ludendorff railway bridge over the Rhine at Remagen was still standing. The local German commander had not yet fulfilled his orders to destroy the bridge, in hopes of using it to continue evacuating his troops.

Grimball's platoon supported the armored infantry and fought their way through town and onto the approaches to the bridge. While the Germans did succeed in using explosives to damage the approach, thereby preventing the tanks from crossing the bridge, the infantry was able to cross and take the bridge, with the T26E3s providing covering file, including demolishing a machine gun nest atop one of the towers on the east bank, as well as destroying the locomotive of an enemy troop train approaching the bridge on the east side.

A T26E3 was destroyed in fighting near Cologne in March, taking an 88 mm round fired point-blank by a Nashorn, causing an ammunition explosion in the American tank. Cologne was, however, also the site of another famous incident involving the T26E3.

A German Panther, in a commanding position in front of the Cologne Cathedral, had knocked out a Sherman and was positioned to continue controlling this key location. A T26E3 from Company E, 32nd Armored Regiment, 3rd Armored Division, under the command of Sgt. Bob Early, was sent to address the Panther. Approaching from the side, gunner Clarence Smoyer fired three rounds in rapid succession at the Panther, igniting the German tank and destroying it.

In March, a second shipment of T26E3s reached Antwerp. These forty tanks were assigned to the 9th Army, with the 2nd Armored Division getting twenty-two of them and the 5th Armored Division receiving eighteen. That same month, the T26E3 was standardized as the M26. Thirty more arrived in April, all going to the 11th Armored Division, 3rd Army. These were the last to see combat in Europe, although by VE-Day a total of 310 T26E3s were in Europe, and two hundred were issued to tank units.

Ordnance also shipped a dozen T26E3s to the Pacific, on the basis of unfortunate encounters with the Japanese 47 mm antitank guns on Okinawa. The big new tanks did not reach Okinawa until July 21, 1945, after the fighting was over. The vehicles were issued to the 193rd and 711th Tank Battalions in preparation of the invasion of the Japanese home islands, but the war ended before that invasion was executed.

The Zebra Mission was a well-organized technical and logistical effort by the US Army and the Fisher Tank Arsenal to prepare and place into action twenty T26E3s in the European theater. Ten tanks each were detailed to the 3rd Armored Division and the 9th Armored Division. After arriving in the port of Antwerp, Belgium, in early February 1945, the tanks were transported to Brussels on 40-ton M25 tank transporters / truck trailers, with the semitrailers modified with bridges over the wheels to accept the wide tracks of the Pershings. *US Army Armor & Cavalry Collection*

A training school was established at Aachen, Germany, to give a crash course in the T26E3 to the crews from the 3rd Armored Division in February 1945. Also at Aachen, the 559th Heavy Maintenance Tank Company prepared the vehicles for combat. Here, the crew of a T26E3 is conducting maneuvers in a field. The turret is in the travel position, with the 90 mm gun tube in the lock, and a cover is over the .50-caliber antiaircraft machine gun. *US Army Armor & Cavalry Collection*

A Pershing, probably the same one in the preceding photo, is negotiating a knoll outside Aachen during crew training in February 1945. The crews from the 3rd Armored Division, specifically from the 32nd and 33rd Armored Regiments, completed all of their instructions on the tanks by February 20. *US Army Armor & Cavalry Collection*

At the T26E3 tank school at Aachen, L. R. "Slim" Price, a civilian technician at Aberdeen Proving Ground and an expert on the tank's 90 mm gun, held classes on gunnery, after which he selected a field near the city for a firing range. There, he guided the crews in boresighting their 90 mm guns, after which they conducted target practice, as seen here in a photo of T26E3 registration number 30119836, serial number 26, assigned to Company E, 33rd Armored Regiment, 3rd Armored Division. Each crew fired twenty-eight rounds, completing these procedures by February 23. The Pershings and their crews now were ready for combat. *US Army Armor & Cavalry Collection*

Members of the crew of T26E3, serial number 40 and registration number 30119850, from Company E, 33rd Armored Regiment, 3rd Armored Division, pose in front of their tank in Elsdorf, Germany. On February 27, 1945, they knocked out a Tiger I and two Pz.Kpfw. IVs in that town. *US Army Armor & Cavalry Collection*

During the advance of the Zebra Mission in Germany, two T26E3s suffered engine failure. Here, a mechanic is preparing for an engine replacement in the field. The rear of the engine is visible to the right of the soldier. The engine exhaust has been removed, exposing the opening for it in the rear of the hull. Lying on the open right ventilating grille/door of the engine compartment is a pair of overshoes. *US Army Armor & Cavalry Collection*

The same operation is viewed from more to the left. To the rear of the tank is part of the apparatus for hoisting the power pack. Under camouflage netting in the background is a shop van, containing machines and equipment for performing field repairs. *US Army Armor & Cavalry Collection*

The first T26E3 lost in combat was a tank nicknamed "FIREBALL," serial number 38 and registration number 30119848, from Company F, 33rd Armored Regiment, which was knocked out at Elsdorf on the night of February 26, 1945. The crew of a Tiger I tank spotted the turret of the Pershing, which was backlit by a fire in the background, and commenced firing at a range of under 100 yards. The third shot fired by the Tiger creased the top of the gun shield. *US Army Armor & Cavalry Collection*

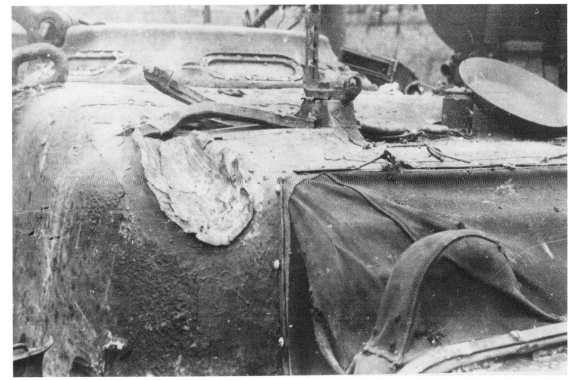

The first round fired by the Tiger I tank at "FIREBALL," a solid-shot projectile, struck and penetrated the gun shield at the coaxial machine gun port, visible here although obscured by tree branches. That shot killed the gunner and the loader; they were the only crewmen killed. The second shot of the Tiger tank struck the muzzle brake of the 90 mm gun of "FIREBALL," rupturing it: it is visible close-up to the left of center. The 88 mm round that grazed the gun shield hit the open hatch door of the commander's cupola, taking out the round, center part of the door, leaving only the frame standing. *US Army Armor & Cavalry Collection*

The hole the 88 mm projectile punched through the coaxial machine-gun port on "FIREBALL" is seen from a closer perspective. Lying on the glacis are the two escape hatches for the driver and the assistant driver / bow gunner. The nickname FIREBALL is stenciled on the sand shield. *US Army Armor & Cavalry Collection*

The impact of the 88 mm projectile that struck the muzzle brake of "FIREBALL" caused a cartridge in the chamber of the 90 mm gun to discharge, causing the gun tube to bulge before the cartridge passed out through the muzzle. The area where the tube bulged is marked by the shiny, bare metal. According to a report of this battle damage, the round that struck the muzzle brake also created the large hole in the upper front of the rack for the drivers' hoods on the right side of the turret. Subsequently, "FIREBALL" was repaired, a new gun scavenged from a 90 mm GMC M36 was installed to replace the original barrel, and the tank was returned to active service on March 7, 1945. *US Army Armor & Cavalry Collection*

"FIREBALL" (Company F, 33rd Armored Regiment, 3rd Armored Division) was one of the most famous T26E3 tanks of the Zebra Mission. On February 26, 1945, this tank was knocked out by a German Tiger at Elsdorf.

FIREBALL

30119848

3Δ-33-Δ   F25

Front view of "FIREBALL"

This T26E3 heavy tank, serial number 22 and registration number 30119832, commanded by Sgt. Chester Key, of Company A, 14th Tank Battalion, 9th Armored Division, was knocked out by two German large-caliber, high-explosive shells at a road intersection east of the Roer River on the night of March 1, 1945. The crew evacuated the tank after the first hit, but Sgt. Key was killed when a second shell hit the right side of the turret to the rear of the commander's cupola. That blast launched the commander's cupola into the air. It is lying, minus its hatch door, on the ground. *US Army Armor & Cavalry Collection*

The first shell to hit Sgt. Key's Pershing detonated near the right sprocket, igniting a fire in the engine compartment, wrecking the right fender and sand shield, and damaging the right sprocket, track, and right-rear bogie wheels. That shell blew a storage box off the fender, and it is lying on the ground to the lower right. *US Army Armor & Cavalry Collection*

The second shell struck the right side of the turret but did not penetrate it. As a result of the two artillery hits, all the bolts that secured the turret to the hull, save four, were severed. This tank was one of the earliest Pershings equipped with T80E1 double-pin tracks. *US Army Armor & Cavalry Collection*

Sgt. Chester Key commanded this Pershing (serial number 22) when it came under night fire on March 1, 1945. Key was killed in action, but the tank later rejoined Company A, 14th Tank Battalion, 9th Armored Division.

Crewmen of a T26E3 from 1st Platoon, Company A, 14th Tank Battalion, 9th Armored Division, are awaiting orders to advance, outside Vettweiss, Germany, on March 1, 1945. Six days later, on March 7, this platoon would play a key role in the capture of the Ludendorff Bridge, at Remagen. *National Archives*

Five of the T26E3s under Zebra Mission served with the 19th Tank Battalion's A, B, and C Companies. This example is advancing along the road from Thum to Ginnick, Germany, on March 1, 1945. A tarpaulin is rolled up on the fender (the T26E3 technical manual called for the storage of a 12 × 12 ft. "paulin" on the left fender), and two drivers' foul-weather hoods are stored in the rack on the side of the turret. In the background is an M32A1 tank recovery vehicle with a mine roller attached. *National Archives*

During the battle for Cologne, Germany, on March 6, 1945, a T26E3 from Company E, 32nd Armored Regiment, part of Task Force X of the 3rd Armored Division, gained renown by winning a duel with a Panther tank in the cathedral square. The Pershing, serial number 26 and registration number 30119836, is seen from the rear as it makes its way along a street with the towers of the cathedral looming in the distance. The last part of the registration number, 836, is clearly visible on the rear of the hull. The commander of this Pershing was Sgt. Bob Earley. *National Archives*

While engaged in vicious street fighting in Cologne, Sgt. Earley learned that a Panther tank was set up in an ambush position in the square in front of the cathedral. Armed with that foreknowledge, he and his crew maneuvered into position near an intersection, out of sight of the Panther's crew. Finally, the tank moved into the intersection, and the gunner, Clarence Smoyer, brought the 90 mm gun to bear on the Panther as the Panther's gunner struggled to bring his gun onto the Pershing. The Panther commander, Wilhelm Bartelborth, ordered his gunner to halt, thinking the nearby tank was German. This gave Smoyer the edge; he fired an armor-piercing round, which struck the Panther's engine compartment. A second round found its mark, and when a third round penetrated the tank, the Panther erupted in flames. *National Archives*

During the advance toward the cathedral of Cologne, a crewman of T26E3, serial number 26, has just tossed a 90 mm shell casing out of a hatch. The registration number was painted on the rear of the hull, with the exhaust and the travel lock splitting the number in two. The "9" in the 30119836 number is hidden by the travel lock.

Sgt. Bob Earley's T26E3 was very well documented photographically during its fight in Cologne on March 6, 1945, including film footage by Jim Bates of the 165th Photo Signal Company, showing, from the upper story of a nearby building, the duel with the Panther tank in the cathedral square and its aftermath. Shortly after the Pershing knocked out the Panther, Bates made his way down to the street and captured a clip of the crew, lasting almost a minute. In this still from the clip are, *left to right,* assistant driver Homer "Smokey" Davis, commander Bob Earley, gunner Clarence Smoyer, driver William McVey, and loader John DeRiggi. *National Archives*

Although 9th Armored Division Pershings participated in the capture of the Ludendorff Bridge at Remagen on March 7, 1945, these tanks were too heavy and wide to cross the Rhine on the damaged bridge. Hence, on March 12 the T26E3s were ferried across the Rhine River at Remagen on barges improvised from pontoon-bridge sections. These ferries transported the Pershings as well as troops and supplies to the eastern shore of the river, under artillery fire. This M26E3 is being maneuvered into position on a barge before crossing the river. *National Archives*

A US Army Corps of Engineers sign announces the builders of a pontoon bridge over the Rhine River, as a T26E3—turret traversed to the rear—begins the passage on the treadways, which were 1,140 feet long. The site was on the west bank of the river opposite Wesel, Germany. The bridge was constructed by the 17th Armored Engineer Battalion in late March 1945 and was near a destroyed bridge, visible in the background. The bridge was designed for heavy vehicles, up to 25 tons, and had a bridge classification of 40, as indicated by the round sign on the stanchion next to the Pershing. *National Archives*

By late March 1945, a new shipment of T26E3s had arrived in the European theater, with the 9th Army receiving forty of them. Of these Pershings, twenty-two were assigned to the 2nd Armored Division, and eighteen to the 5th Armored Division. A building is afire as a column of Pershings are on the march to join the 2nd Armored Division outside Wesel, Germany, on March 30, 1945. *National Archives*

The 11th Armored Division also received T26E3s in the final days of World War II in Germany. This example is leading a group of German prisoners of war to a detention center. Two spare bogie wheels are stored on the glacis, and knapsacks and other gear are hanging from the turret.

Prompted by the heavy losses of Sherman tanks in the Okinawa campaign (a total of 221 US Army tanks were knocked out on the island by the end of May 1945, with ninety-four listed as beyond repair), the Army detailed Capt. Elmer Gray, who had been a principal member of the Zebra Mission in Germany, to lead a similar mission to train tankers on Okinawa in the operation and maintenance of the new Pershing tanks. Twelve Pershings departed from Mukiltea, Washington, on SS *Katherine D. Sherwood* on May 31, but many delays ensued, and by the time the transport arrived at Naha, Okinawa, on July 21, hostilities had ended on Okinawa. However, at that time, an invasion of Japan in the fall of 1945 was scheduled, and the Pershings would be needed in that conflict. Unloading of the Pershings from SS *Katherine D. Sherwood* at Naha, as seen here, began on July 30. The front and presumably the rear brackets for an engine hoist have been removed from the left side of the turret.

The Pershings delivered by SS *Katherine D. Sherwood* were unloaded onto LCTs (landing craft, tanks) off Naha on July 30, 1945, and were landed on a beach the following day. This is one of the first vehicles landed on July 31. After the fourth Pershing landed, operations were postponed because of typhoon warnings. The remaining eight tanks were landed at Naha on August 4. The tanks were equally apportioned to the 193rd and 711th Tank Battalions.

The T26E3 was standardized as the M26 in March 1945. This example, whose partially hidden registration number—stenciled on the hull below the engine exhaust and on the center storage box— seems to be 30128627S (the "S" certifying that the vehicle was adequately shielded from radio interference), is secured to the deck of the battleship USS *Arkansas* (BB-33) on May 2, 1946. The tank and the ship were destined for the nuclear tests at Bikini Atoll in the Pacific in July of that year. *National Archives*

OFFICE CHIEF OF ORDNANCE-DETROIT
NEG. No. 6388   DATE 5-23-45   DEVELOPMENT DIV.
Tank, Heavy, M26. 3/4 right front view.

The Pershings were redesignated from heavy to medium tanks after World War II. This photograph, taken on May 23, 1945, two weeks after the surrender of Germany and almost three months before Japan announced its surrender, bears an original label identifying it as a "Tank, Heavy, M26." The faintly visible registration on the ventilator bulge, 301272959 S, is puzzling, since it has one digit more than the T26E3/M26 registration numbers published by the US Army in World War II. *TACOM LCMC History Office*

CHAPTER 3
The Pershing Up Close

Prominently displayed at the Wright Museum of World War II in Wolfeboro, New Hampshire, is Fisher T26E3, serial number 35—one of the tanks involved in taking the Remagen Bridge in Germany on March 7, 1945.

The Pershing's idler wheel position used the same wheels and bearings as the six road wheel stations on each side, which simplified logistics.

The idler wheel was attached to the front road wheel arm. This placement allowed the idler wheel and first road wheel to work together to maintain correct track tension when traversing uneven terrain. *US Army via Scott Taylor*

The substantial construction of the suspension components as well as the reverse side of the road wheel installation is clearly shown. For six decades, other US tanks used similar suspension systems.

Five dual track support rollers were mounted on each side. Twelve bolts attached each pair of support rollers to the hub.

Most, if not all, of the double-pin-type track-equipped tanks on the Zebra Mission used this type of drive sprocket. This is the drive sprocket of the tank from Sgt. Chester Key's Company A, 14th Tank Battalion, 9th Armored Division, the tank in which he was killed in night battle on March, 1, 1945, just east of the Roer River. The damage shown was incurred during that action. *Patton Museum*

Although less elaborate, a sprocket similar to the TM illustration was found on some of the Pershings in the Korean conflict. Lower production cost was a factor in this design.

This very simple drive sprocket design became commonplace, and many of the Pershings operating in Korea had these simple sprockets.

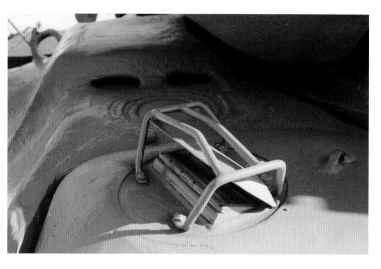

The earliest Pershings had a 400 cfm (cubic feet per minute) RotoClone hull ventilation blower located between the driver's and assistant driver's hatches. The glacis plate had a rounded area near the hull top. Initially, hull-mounted periscopes were placed on either side of the blower casing. *Rob Ervin*

The initial production tanks had four M6 periscopes installed in the drivers' compartment. One periscope was placed in each hatch, and one periscope was placed between each hatch and the blower housing. *Rory Clarke*

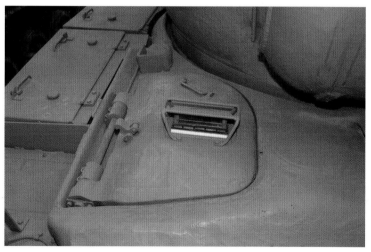

Periscopes mounted in the driver's and assistant driver's hatches continued to provide the drivers with forward vision. The hull periscope position has a welded-in plug on this tank. *Chris Hughes*

These periscopes were considered a vulnerability. On later-production vehicles, the periscope mounting points were plated over. Two circular plates (visible ahead of the turret) are evidence of this change. *Chris Hughes*

The 400 cfm blower proved inadequate. Beginning with the Fisher serial number 550 tank and the Chrysler serial number 235 tank, the Pershings received a 1,000 cfm unit. The new blower necessitated a redesign of the front hull casting, which resulted in a much-flatter but broader hump in the glacis plate.

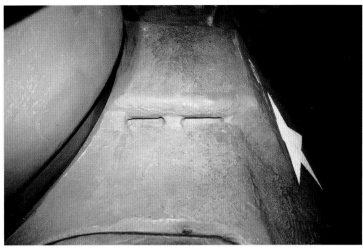

Later tanks with the 1,000 cfm blower had no provision for the hull-mounted driver's and assistant driver's periscopes. Hence, the armored top of the drivers' compartment was a solid, uninterrupted casting that offered better armor protection.

The depressions used for the hull-mounted periscopes on tanks with 400 cfm blowers gave the impression that the blower housings were raised higher than the 1,000 cfm blower-equipped tanks. In the foreground, the latch on the assistant driver's hatch is used to secure the hatch when it is open.

Though they had their own foundry for large armor components, the Fisher Body Division of General Motors used outside vendors. The lower, front armor casting on this Fisher-built Pershing was produced by General Steel Casting Corporation, and the foundry's markings were formed into the piece.

Eight hinged, louvered doors covered the engine and transmission and permitted cool air to circulate through the radiator. The armor plate that crosses the tank protects the radiator. Forward of the radiator, air draws in. The air flows out as exhaust toward the rear of the tank.

The Pershing's cooling system consisted of two radiators that held a combined total of 22 gallons of coolant. Four engine-driven, five-blade fans circulated air through these grilles.

The forward stowage compartment on the driver's side housed an M3 tripod with pintle. This equipment was used for dismounted operation of either of the two .30-caliber M1919A4 machine guns or the M2 HB .50-caliber machine gun. *Chris Hughes*

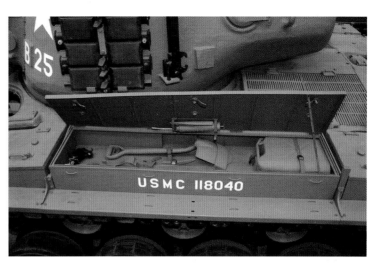

The center stowage compartment on the driver's side held a 5-gallon water can, pioneer tools, a grease gun, the wrench used for adjusting track tension, and an inspection light with a 15-foot cord that could be plugged into the tank's electrical system. *Chris Hughes*

An 18-quart folding canvas bucket and personal items, such as bedrolls, were stowed in the rear compartment. The holes below the compartment latches are vents that prevent condensation from forming in these compartments. *Chris Hughes*

When viewed from the outside, these vents appear as knobs. Rising above the toolbox lid's outer edges are two supports for the engine compartment grilles when the compartment is open.

This M26A1, owned by the Military Vehicle Technology Foundation, shows how parts can be mixed during repairs and rebuilding. A "smooth" fender is installed on the left side, and a ribbed fender is installed on the right side. The box above the right blackout taillight houses a telephone-type handset for communication between the tank crew and the infantry, which was a post–World War II addition. The tank rides on a steel T80E1 track, and the pintle hook is in the stowed position. *Chris Hughes*

A cam-type latch mechanism held the cover on the interphone box. The right-rear fender brace runs behind the telephone box mounting plate. *Chris Hughes*

The RC-298 interphone extension kit consisted of the BC-1362 external interphone box and switch box BC-1361, which included the H-22 handset. Such communication abilities were critical for coordination of armor with supporting infantry. *Chris Hughes*

The interphone box has been removed from this tank, but the mounting plate for the box remains. The towing pintle is in place. The Pershing tanks were not typically used for towing. So, the pintle was normally stowed in order to improve the angle of departure when traversing rough terrain.

The interphone box mounting was made from heavy steel plate, as evident here. A substantial steel lifting ring was welded on the tank's right rear. The Pershing manual warned against lifting the tank from any points other than these rings and their counterparts on the tank's front.

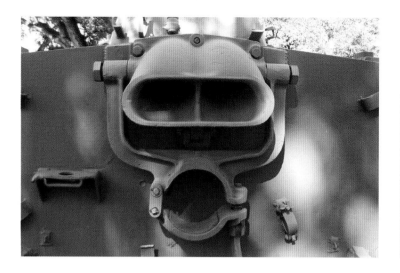

On the earliest-production Pershings, the main gun travel-lock mounting was integral with the engine exhaust casing. Once in the field, troops discovered this mounting placed too much stress on the exhaust outlet and caused it to crack. *Rory Clarke*

To alleviate this problem, the travel lock's mounting lugs were welded to the rear hull. A fabric lining was present inside the actual clamp portion of the travel lock. This lining prevented metal-to-metal contact with the gun tube.

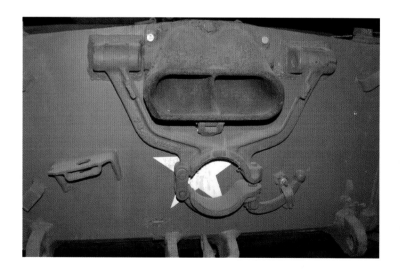

The travel lock was not always mounted symmetrically around the exhaust outlet. On this tank, someone has secured the travel-lock handle in the clamp designed to hold one end of the tow cable.

Tanks rebuilt as M26A1 tanks had their travel locks relocated to a position on the engine deck. This relocation cleared the area around the exhaust outlet completely. *Chris Hughes*

The right-rear stowage compartment held blankets and part of the crew's rations. Prescribed stowage for the tank's five-man crew was a two-day supply, which consisted of sixty cans of C rations or thirty boxes of K rations.

A 10-pound sledgehammer, an M1942 field stove (the shiny can object on the left), and an identification panel set were some of the items stored in the right-side center stowage compartment.

The stowage box lids had reinforcements spot-welded to the underside, which permitted the lids to act as walkways. To secure the camouflage net, footman loops were placed along the boxes' outer vertical surfaces and fender tops.

The right-side front stowage compartment was divided into several smaller compartments. A decontaminator, wire cutters, and track pin tools were some of the items placed in this stowage compartment.

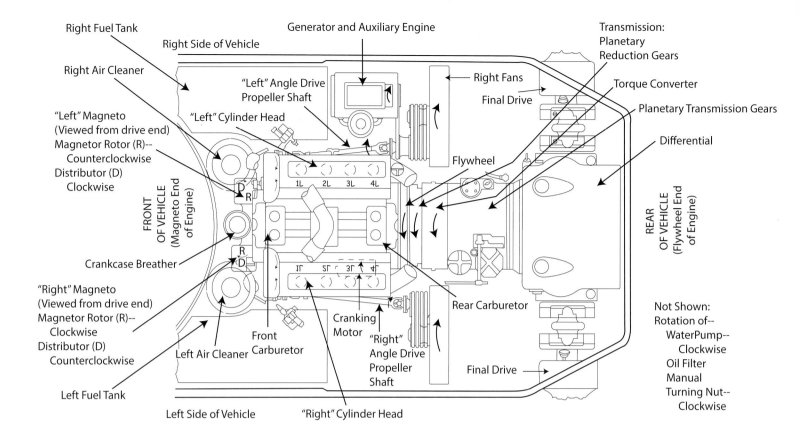

Right Fuel Tank

Right Side of Vehicle

Generator and Auxiliary Engine

Transmission:
Planetary
Reduction Gears

Right Air Cleaner

Right Fans

Torque Converter

"Left" Angle Drive
Propeller Shaft

Final Drive

Planetary Transmission Gears

"Left" Cylinder Head

"Left" Magneto
(Viewed from drive end)
Magnetor Rotor (R)--
Counterclockwise
Distributor (D)
Clockwise

Differential

Flywheel

1L   2L   3L   4L

FRONT
OF VEHICLE
(Magneto End
of Engine)

REAR
OF VEHICLE
(Flywheel End
of Engine)

D   R

R
D

Crankcase Breather

Rear Carburetor

"Right" Magneto
(Viewed from drive end)
Magnetor Rotor (R)--
Clockwise
Distributor (D)
Counterclockwise

Not Shown:
Rotation of--
WaterPump--
Clockwise
Oil Filter
Manual
Turning Nut--
Clockwise

Cranking
Motor

Left Air Cleaner

Front
Carburetor

1L   5L   3L   4L

"Right"
Angle Drive
Propeller
Shaft

Final Drive

Left Fuel Tank

Left Side of Vehicle

"Right" Cylinder Head

Although not accurately scaled, this reproduction drawing from a technical manual drawing gives the
overall layout of the Pershing's engine transmission compartment.

The Ford GAF engine, which was developed from the Ford GAA in the photo, powered the Pershing. The GAF had different exhaust manifolds and differed in other details.

Like the GAA, the GAF had dual two-barrel downdraft carburetors. The 1,100-cubic-inch displacement GAF required a minimum of 80-octane fuel and developed 500 net horsepower.

The engine was a 60-degree V-8 with 5.4-inch bore and 6-inch stroke. The engine originated from an aborted Ford aircraft engine design. The engine developed 1,040 lbs. per foot of torque. However, the Pershing was underpowered even with this much horsepower.

The left side of the engine compartment of a T26E3 is shown, with the left rear of the turret bustle to the upper left. The side of the Ford GAF V-8 gasoline engine is in view, including the left cylinder head and exhaust manifold. Below the exhaust manifold is the propeller shaft for the left fan. Above the engine, the left branch of the carburetor air-intake tube passes through a cutout in a shield.

In the right side of the engine compartment is the right branch of the carburetor air-intake tube, as well as the right cylinder head and exhaust manifold. In the front of the compartment is an expanded-steel-mesh guard over several components mounted atop the right fuel tank. The red T-handle of the engine-oil dipstick is next to the cylinder head. To the rear of the cylinder head is the red cap for the oil filler.

More details of the right side of the engine compartment are shown, along with the open compartment door / ventilation grille to the right. The red object below the steel-mesh guard is a fire-extinguisher nozzle. In the background to the left is the armored cover for the radiator water filler.

The five-blade, belt-driven cooling fans on the left side of the tank pushed air through one radiator. A similar set of fans on the right side cooled the other radiator.

To the rear of the engine compartment of the T26E3/M26 is the controlled-type differential, shown with the door/ventilator grilles open. The controlled differential transmitted power from the engine and transmission to the final drives, and it also contained brakes for stopping the vehicle as well as steering it by varying the speeds of the two tracks. Not in view to the front of the differential is the Torqmatic transmission.

This view from the upper rear shows the engine-compartment doors, which doubled as ventilation grilles, open, revealing the controlled differential in the rear. The right fuel tank is in the front right corner of the engine compartment, below the right side of the turret bustle.

A-27

Details of the top of the turret of the Wright Museum's T26E3 are displayed. Two antenna base units are installed; to the right of the forward antenna base is the pedestal for a .50-caliber antiaircraft machine gun. To the rear of the pedestal are casting marks: "D7054408" over "SER [serial number] 162" over the trademark of General Steel Castings Corporation.

A rack was made to hold the drivers' hoods when they were not in use. This rack was placed on the right side of the turret. The turret's relatively rough texture resulted from the casting process.

The Pershing's turret was based on the turret developed for the T25 and was made from cast homogeneous steel. An M2 HB .50-caliber machine gun was installed on the turret roof for the commander to use in antiaircraft work. *Chris Hughes*

Two SCD-1241 antennas protrude from the turret roof. The antenna at the turret's rear is for the SCR-528 set, and the antenna near the loader's hatch is connected to an AN/VRC-3 set. *Chris Hughes*

An M26A1 medium tank was photographed while in the collection of the late Jacques Littlefield. It bears replica USMC markings, including registration 118040 on the center storage box on the fender. The distinctive single-baffle muzzle brake and bore extractor that were features of the M26A1 are present. A track jack is stored on its brackets above the lifting eye on the side of the turret bustle. *Chris Hughes*

Two oblong vents are visible on the ventilator hood between the drivers' hatches. The tracks are the type T80E1, a double-pin design with chevron grousers on the steel shoes. The bogie wheels, the track-return rollers, and the idlers all had rubber tires. *Chris Hughes*

A socket was provided on the turret's rear to allow the .50-caliber machine gun to be stowed. The socket accepted the machine gun mount's pintle and cradle.

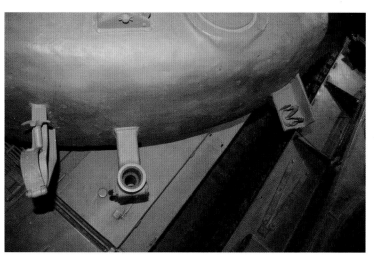

The clamp to the left was secured around the barrel support on the machine gun's receiver. The clamp completed the machine gun's stowage and held it firmly in place.

A track-connecting fixture or track jack was stored to the rear of the hood stowage rack. Two track jacks were needed to repair or replace the vehicle's tracks.

This device used a simple screw mechanism to pull the ends of the track runs together. Bolts were used to close the stowage bracket since it did not require rapid access.

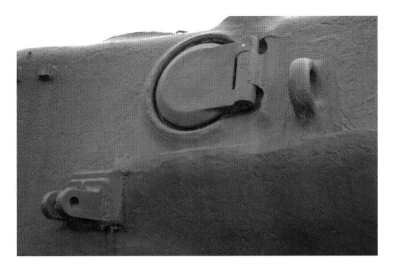

A pistol port was located in the turret's left wall. The bracket below and to the left of the pistol port was intended to attach an engine-lifting fixture. However, the lifting-fixture brackets were found only on the earliest-production tanks.

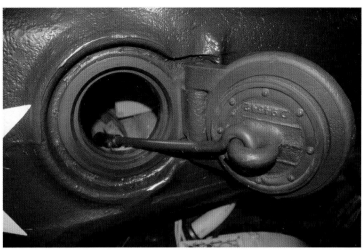

The pistol port door was sealed with a gasket to prevent water from entering the turret.

Forward of the pistol port and adjacent to the spare track links are brackets for storing the second track-connecting fixture. The spare track sections were not continuous. Instead, they consisted of two two-link sections.

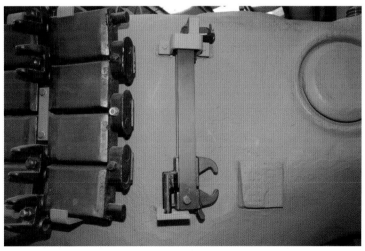

The track jack firmly bolts into its stowage brackets. The inner, rubber-covered surface of the track links was an effort to quiet the tank's operation. The former locations of both engine-lifting hoist brackets are visible in this photo. One area is near the mantlet, and the other area is near the pistol port.

The forward lifting-mechanism bracket on early tanks' turrets was located near the trunnion cover mounting.

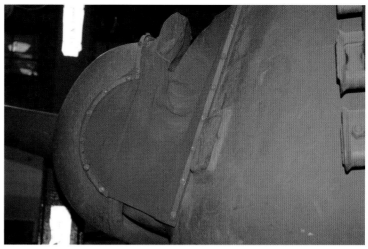

A canvas cover protected the mantlet and turret junction on service tanks. This cover kept debris such as limbs, brass, and stones from jamming the elevating mechanism.

The T26E3 Pershing's M3 90 mm gun was equipped with a double-baffle muzzle brake. This brake reduced recoil force and freed up space in the turret's cramped interior. The rear baffle of the muzzle brake featured a replaceable bushing in the bore. The entire muzzle brake was screwed onto the gun tube.

The M26A1 was armed with the improved M3A1 90 mm cannon. When this weapon was created, the outer baffle of the M3's muzzle brake was removed. Also, a bore evacuator was installed and is located just behind the muzzle brake.

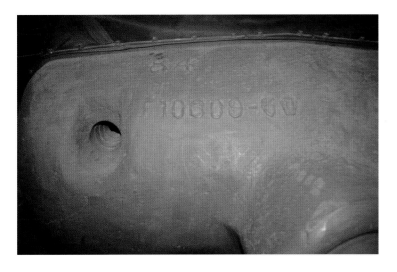

The Pershing had a large cast gun mantlet, which was one of the most vulnerable areas on the tank. One reason for this vulnerability was the direct-sight telescope aperture, which is visible in the photo to the left of the foundry markings.

An opening for the M1919A4 coaxial machine gun was placed on the left side of the mantlet and was another vulnerable area.

The canvas trunnion cover extended the full width of the mantlet and included pockets to cover the mantlet's lifting rings and the separate turret front.

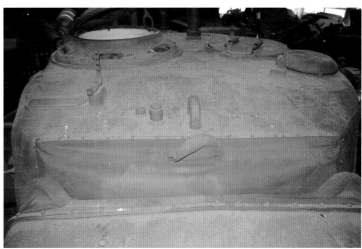

The commander's sighting vane was placed just inboard of the gunner's M10F periscope. The plug between the sighting vane and the forward turret-lifting ring was the mounting point for the spotlight.

A Browning M2 heavy-barrel .50-caliber machine gun was mounted on the turret roof for antiaircraft and close-in defense use. The M2 had a maximum range of 7,000 yards. However, its effective range was closer to 2,000 yards. *Chris Hughes*

The M2 Browning or "Ma Deuce" can fire 450 to 550 rounds per minute. The Pershing's mounting pedestal is hinged and allows a modest height reduction. *Chris Hughes*

This antiaircraft machine gun mount has its pintle and cradle in place. Originally known as the D80030 pintle assembly, the mount was later designated the 6580030 mount assembly and was made from cast steel. This gun mount has the 7046650 ammo box holder.

An M6 periscope was mounted in the center of the commander's cupola. While other M6 periscopes on the tank rotated in their own mount, this periscope is fixed rigidly to the commander's hatch. However, the entire center portion of the hatch rotated.

The inner surface of the commander's hatch was also painted Olive Drab, and part of the surface was covered with black padding. A soft black pad also ringed the cupola opening. *Chris Hughes*

Around the outer circumference of the cupola hatch was an azimuth scale. This scale could be used in conjunction with the vane sight, which was located just ahead of the commander's periscope. *Chris Hughes*

The inner surface on the loader's hatch that was not covered with a black pad was painted olive drab.

This view is of the commander's cupola from inside the tank. An M15A1 periscope has been installed instead of the specified M6. Typically, the M15A1 periscope was associated with the M46 rather than the Pershing.

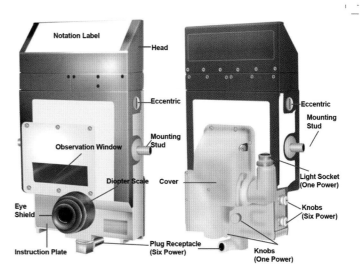

The prescribed M10F periscope had two built-in optical systems. A single-power system was for general observation, and a six-power system was for gunlaying on distant targets. This illustration lists the primary components of the M10F.

The gunner was furnished with an M10F periscope, which connected to the gun-elevating mechanism. The periscope allowed the gunner to see where his gun was aimed. This particular tank was refitted with the similar M16F periscope.

The linkage between the periscope and the gun-elevating mechanism tilted the periscope as the gun was elevated or depressed. In the foreground is one of three turret compartment lamps, with red and white bulbs.

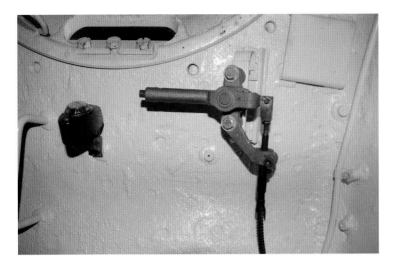

On the turret's roof, the Hull compass was placed just to the left of the commander's bronze-colored, turret traverse control. The button on the end of the traverse control lever had to be depressed to move the lever as a safeguard.

The turret master switch box hangs on the right turret wall near the commander's seat. This box turns on the power to the electric motor, which drives the hydraulic pump for traversing the turret.

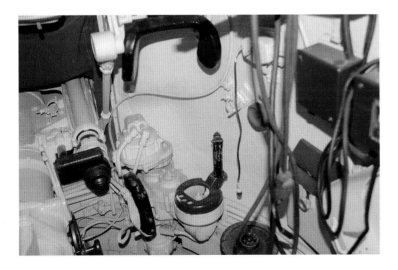

To the far left in this photo of the gunner's position is the right side of the breech. The direct-sight telescope is aligned with the main gun mounting, and to the right is the black hydraulic turret traverse control lever with coaxial machine gun trigger. The red object is the manual turret traverse control lever, and the black object at the top of the photo is the gunner's headrest, which aligned with his periscope.

The azimuth indicator was positioned beside the gunner's seat. This indicator provided the position of the gun when it was traversed. The turret ring gear drove the azimuth indicator, which was illuminated by dry-cell batteries.

The turret traverse safety lock is near the bottom of the photo and is highlighted with red paint. This safety lock was a manually operated mechanism that inserted a pawl into the turret ring gear to prevent the turret from being traversed hydraulically or manually.

The manual turret traverse mechanism engages the turret ring gear.

The gunner used an M71C telescope that was mounted beside the cannon with a T90 telescope mount. This telescope was engineered for sighting direct fire.

The elevating handwheel sat below the gun cradle. Gun elevation and depression were manual, and the gun had a range of elevation from –10 to +20 degrees.

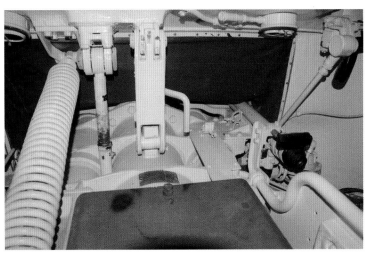

The internal travel lock folded against the turret roof when not in use. To use the turret gun travel lock, the gunner swung the device down until it engaged a hook cast into the gun cradle assembly.

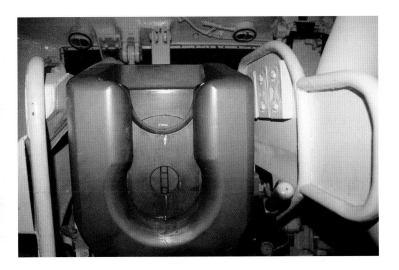

The breech ring was screwed onto the end of the gun tube. The breechblock lifted vertically during operation. The lever on the right controlled breechblock lifting.

Weights were attached to the inner surface off the recoil guard to help balance the weapon. The turret switch box, pictured here with its protective guard, is beneath the step on the turret wall.

Mounted on the left turret wall are the main gun ammunition ready racks that hold ten rounds. The loader's interphone control box is above the rounds. In the turret roof is the loader's periscope. US ammunition with Olive Drab bodies typically denote high-explosive rounds, while black bodies indicate armor-piercing rounds. *Chris Hughes*

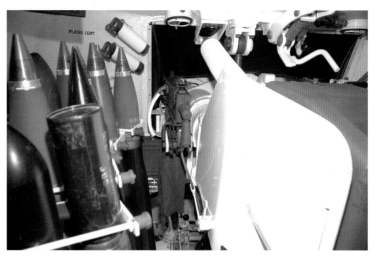

A coaxial M1919A4 .30-caliber Browning machine gun was mounted on the left side of the main gun. A canvas bag was suspended from the weapon to catch the spent brass. *Chris Hughes*

The coaxial weapon was fed from an ammo box placed below and to the left of the machine gun. Although normally fired electrically by a trigger located on top of the hydraulic traverse control handle (the main gun trigger was to the front of the same handle), the gunner could also fire the machine manually by pulling the trigger at the rear of the weapon. *Chris Hughes*

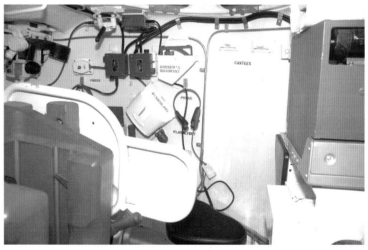

Like all armored vehicles, the Pershing's interior was cramped. This view, taken from the loader's seat, shows the commander's and gunner's positions. To the right of the photo is the edge of the radio set. Three interphone control boxes are visible. Two of the boxes are on the right turret wall. Another control box is mounted on the turret roof. *Chris Hughes*

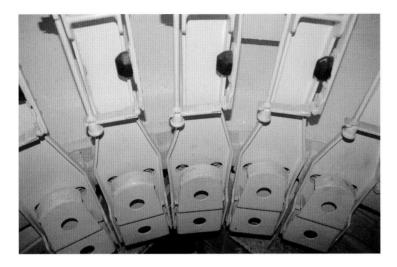

As the ammunition ready racks were emptied, the upper supports dropped to allow easy access to the next two-round rack, and the ready racks' lower portion folded up when not in use. Each 90 mm round weighed between 23 and 24 pounds and was handled with care.

Interleaved sheet-steel shelves supported the ammunition in the wet racks (deemed "wet" because they were flooded with water to minimize fire-induced explosion risk). During lulls in action, ammunition was redistributed to the ready racks from the wet-stowage boxes in the floor.

The main wet-ammunition-stowage racks were in the tank's floor. The four floor racks held a combined sixty rounds of 90 mm ammunition.

The pistol port door is open in this picture. To the left of the door are stowage racks for 550 rounds of .50-caliber machine gun ammunition, several boxes of .30-caliber ammunition, various clips of .45-caliber ammunition, twelve hand grenades, and various tools and supplies needed for the tank and crew.

On the other side of the turret bustle is the SCR-528 radio set. The radio is mounted lengthwise of the tank. Above the radio is a compartment light, and beside the radio, on the turret wall, is a retractable extension cable and handle that allows the commander to use the floodlight as a handheld spotlight. *Chris Hughes*

The SCR-528 was the standard tactical vehicle during World War II. The 200-pound set operated at 20.0 to 27.9 MHz and had a BC-602 transmitter, a BC-603 receiver, a BC-605 interphone, and two dynamotors. The ten-tube, 20-watt BC-604 had a 10-mile maximum range.

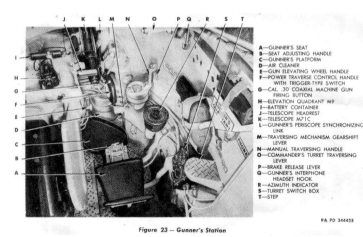

Figure 23 – Gunner's Station

A—GUNNER'S SEAT
B—SEAT ADJUSTING HANDLE
C—GUNNER'S PLATFORM
D—AIR CLEANER
E—GUN ELEVATING WHEEL HANDLE
F—POWER TRAVERSE CONTROL HANDLE WITH TRIGGER-TYPE SWITCH
G—CAL. .30 COAXIAL MACHINE GUN FIRING BUTTON
H—ELEVATION QUADRANT M9
I—BATTERY CONTAINER
J—TELESCOPE HEADREST
K—TELESCOPE M71C
L—GUNNER'S PERISCOPE SYNCHRONIZING LINK
M—TRAVERSING MECHANISM GEARSHIFT LEVER
N—MANUAL TRAVERSING HANDLE
O—COMMANDER'S TURRET TRAVERSING LEVER
P—BRAKE RELEASE LEVER
Q—GUNNER'S INTERPHONE HEADSET HOOK
R—AZIMUTH INDICATOR
S—TURRET SWITCH BOX
T—STEP

RA PD 344455

The general arrangement of the gunner's seat and his position is shown in this technical-manual illustration. The rear of the gunner's seat was quickly removable, which allowed the gunner to get in and out of his seat.

Like the driver, the assistant driver always had an M6 periscope in his hatch. Inboard from and adjacent to the periscope is a small release handle. This handle released the catch that held the hatch open so the hatch could close. *Chris Hughes*

Directly ahead of the assistant driver is the ball-mounted bow machine gun, a .30-caliber Browning M1919A4. Aiming was crude and was accomplished by watching shot placement through the periscope. A canvas bag was provided to catch spent shell casings that otherwise would litter the floor and possibly foul controls. *Chris Hughes*

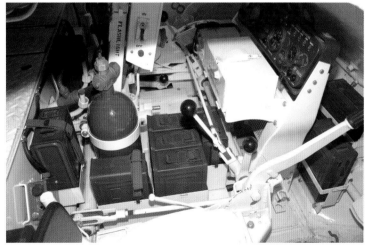

To the right and slightly behind the assistant driver's seat, spare machine gun barrels and one of the four .45-caliber M3 submachine guns were stowed. The submachine guns were part of the tank's on-vehicle material. The M3's maximum rate of fire was 450 rounds per minute, but its practical rate of fire was a third of the maximum. Command tanks were also supplied with a .30-caliber M1 carbine. *Chris Hughes*

Several .30-caliber ammunition boxes were stowed between the assistant driver and driver. The assistant driver's interphone box was located behind the left side of his seat. The instrument panel was positioned between both drivers to allow either one to monitor the vehicle's operation. *Chris Hughes*

The driver's position was on the left front of the hull. His hatch was similar to the codriver's hatch. The padding was positioned directly over crew members' heads. An M3 submachine gun, known as the "Grease Gun," was stowed to the driver's left. *Chris Hughes*

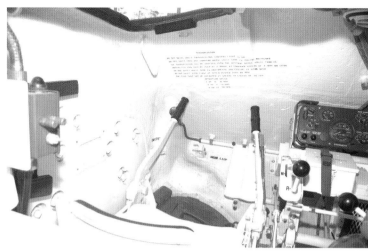

Basic transmission warnings were stenciled on the inner hull in front of the driver. At the right of this photo and the driver's seat is the transmission range selector lever. A linkage connects this control to a similar one on the assistant driver's left. *Chris Hughes*

A pair of fixed fire-extinguisher bottles were mounted between the driver and assistant driver. The personnel heater was located beneath the instrument panel. The Torqmatic transmission made the Pershing easier to drive than most trucks of the period. *Chris Hughes*

The electrical master switch box was mounted to the right of the driver. The 24-volt switch was for vehicle power, and the 12-volt switch was for radio power. At the front of the box was a slave receptacle. All of these items are painted red in this example.

CHAPTER 4
Pershing Variants

Beyond the T26E3, only one other variant of the T26 series would see combat during World War II. Despite numerous T26E2s armed with 105 mm howitzers having been ordered, none of those would see combat until Korea. However, the original T26E1 was sent to Europe. Rearmed with a long-barreled T15E1 90 mm gun using two-part ammunition, this vehicle was intended to be able to go toe to toe with the German King Tiger. While the cannon was impressive, when the tank arrived in Europe the men of the 3rd Armored Division decided it needed additional armor, and cobbled together additional armor for the mantlet and front of the hull—to the tune of 5 tons, considerably overloading the suspension and the tank in general. The formidable "Super Pershing," as it was later known, saw combat only once—knocking out a Panther at 1,500 yards on April 4, 1945, near the Weser River.

An improved version of that same gun, the T15, was the main armament of the limited-production T26E4. Twenty-five examples of this tank were built in 1945, with the contractor modifying the standard T26E3 turret casting to accommodate the more powerful gun.

While the vehicles mentioned previously in this chapter focused on improving the weaponry of the vehicle, the T26E5 sought to improve protection of the vehicle. The thickness of the armor on the hull front was increased to 152 mm, and on the turret front to 190 mm. Beginning in June 1945, twenty-seven examples of the T26E5 were produced.

The T26E2, the vehicle armed with the howitzer, was created specifically to foster the "combat team" approach, which called for a common chassis to be used within a unit. It was intended that the T26E2 be assigned to the headquarters company of T26E3 units.

Drawings were released to Fisher and Chrysler in October 1944, with Fisher constructing the first turret, which was to be mounted on a chassis built by Chrysler. However, due to declining interest, the project lost momentum, and it was July 1945 before the T26E2 pilot was delivered to Aberdeen Proving Ground. Although both Fisher and Chrysler had been contracted to produce complete T26E2 vehicles, after the war in Europe ended, the Fisher contract was canceled and Chrysler's cut back. Production began at Detroit Tank Arsenal in July 1945 and ceased at 185 vehicles. The T26E2 was subsequently standardized as the M45.

In order to defeat the increasingly heavy armor on German panzers and counter the highly potent 88 mm KwK 36 gun in the Tiger II tanks, Aberdeen Proving Ground adapted the new T15E1 90 mm gun. This piece had a muzzle velocity of up to 3,700 feet per second: much higher than that of the M3 90 mm gun of the T26E3 heavy tank and capable of penetrating the frontal armor of Panther tanks at up to 2,600 yards. A T15E1 90 mm gun was tested in the first T26E1 heavy tank, registration number 30103292. Because of the length and weight of the gun tube, a spring equilibrator was required to counterbalance it. Brackets for the equilibrator were welded to the turret roof and the gun shield, as seen in a photo of the tank with the T15E1 90 mm gun at Aberdeen on January 22, 1945. This vehicle was designated as the first of two temporary pilot T26E4 heavy tanks.

The T15E1 90 mm gun required a fixed cartridge 50 inches long, which proved to be very awkward to load in the gun in the confines of the Pershing. Thus, the T15E1 was rechambered to accept a separate projectile and cartridge case and was redesignated the T15E2 90 mm gun. This weapon was installed in the second temporary pilot T26E4 heavy tank, based on T26E3 serial number 97 and registration number 30119907. As seen in an August 3, 1945, photo at Aberdeen Proving Ground, this vehicle had two equilibrator springs in protective cylinders, attached to the turret roof to the front of the commander's cupola and to the right side of the gun shield.

Both of the temporary pilot T26E4s had a weight welded to the rear of the turret bustle, to counterbalance the front-heavy 90 mm gun tube. As seen in an August 4, 1945, view of the second temporary pilot, the underside of the weight actually comprised four separate braces, with their bottoms all curved similarly, although the details are difficult to discern in the shadows.

After testing, the first T26E1 heavy tank (registration number 30103292) with the T15E1 90 mm gun installed, designated the T26E4 heavy tank, temporary pilot no. 1, was shipped to the 3rd Armored Division in the European theater. There, Company C, 3rd Ordnance Maintenance Battalion, then based at Bergheim, Germany, received the tank on March 15, 1945, and proceeded to install additional protection on its front. This included a plate of 80 mm armor from the glacis of a Panther tank, weighing 1,400 pounds, welded to the front of the gun shield, and spaced plate armor on the bow. This tank was dubbed the "Super Pershing."

This tank is T26E4 pilot number 1 as it appeared during trials at Aberdeen Proving Ground in January 1945. This tank was later shipped to Europe for field trials, and its appearance in theater differed considerably from its as-built configuration.

Before the no. 1 temporary pilot T26E4 left the United States for Europe, the original single-spring equilibrator was removed, and a new equilibrator with two coil springs in separate cylinders was substituted. The weight of the extra armor and the long 90 mm gun tube made for a front-heavy vehicle. After Company C, 3rd Maintenance Battalion, prepped the tank, the vehicle served in combat with Company I, 33rd Armored Regiment, 3rd Armored Division, part of Task Force Welborn, during the drive into Germany. Under a dustcover to the front of the loader's hatch is a .50-caliber machine gun.

A side view of the left front of the no. 1 temporary pilot T26E4 heavy tank, as modified by the 3rd Maintenance Battalion, shows the spaced plates installed over the original bow of the tank. This consisted of an inner and an outer structure, both of which were V-shaped, of welded 1.5-inch plates, designed to defeat armor-piercing projectiles. The new glacis was at an angle of 30 degrees from horizontal. The purpose of this spaced armor was to cause projectiles to ricochet or explode outside the hull, rather than penetrate the hull.

A final view of the bow of the no. 1 temporary pilot T26E4 shows details such as towing eyes, a lifting eye near the center of the glacis, and a rack, made of sheet-steel strips, which had been flattened.

The right side of the additional bow armor is viewed close-up, showing the outer plates and, several inches behind them, the inner plates. To the upper right, in a recess in the armor plates, is the ball mount for the coaxial machine gun.

Since the external equilibrator for the T15E2 90 mm gun was vulnerable as well as crucial for the proper operation of the gun, that unit was replaced by a hydropneumatic equilibrator housed in the turret, as development of the T26E4 proceeded. Seen here at Aberdeen Proving Ground on January 2, 1946, is the production pilot T26E4, converted from T26E3 serial number 84 and registration number 30119894, with the equilibrator contained in the turret. A new counterweight was incorporated on the rear of the turret.

The production pilot T26E4, serial number 84, is viewed from above at Aberdeen on January 2, 1946. Except for the long gun tube and the counterweight on the rear of the turret, the vehicle appears to be identical to an early-production T26E3. Drivers' hoods are in the rack on the right side of the turret.

The registration of the T26E4 production pilot 30119894 is present on the ventilator bulge at the top of the glacis, at Aberdeen Proving Ground. A total of fifty-four rounds of 90 mm ammunition were carried. Traverse of the turret was by hydraulic power, and the elevation mechanism of the 90 mm gun and the coaxial machine gun was not stabilized.

A total of twenty-five production T26E4s were completed, all at the Fisher Tank Arsenal. This example is being tested by the Armored Board at Fort Knox, Kentucky; the registration number is not visible. The gun is shown at maximum elevation, 20 degrees. At the front of the turret roof is a spotlight, tilted down.

The minimum elevation of the 90 mm gun of the T26E4, –10 degrees, is demonstrated in this view at Fort Knox.

The same T26E4 is shown in travel disposition, with the turret traversed to the rear and the 90 mm gun tube secured in the travel lock. Largely because of the inconvenience of the separate 90 mm projectiles and propellant casings, the Army exhibited little interest in the T26E4, and production ceased after the first twenty-five vehicles were completed.

Despite an initial order for a thousand of these tanks, decision makers felt a new turret casting was not warranted. Thus, normal-production T26E3 turret castings were modified for use on the T26E4. Beyond the gun tube's additional length, the key identifying feature of the T26E4 was the large counterweight welded to the turret bustle. *Scott Taylor*

Stowage brackets for the M2 .50-caliber machine gun were normally located on the rear of the turret bustle. However, these brackets were relocated to the rear of the counterweight on the T26E4. *Scott Taylor*

The heavy weld beads are indicative of the need to preserve armor protection while simultaneously joining two large steel castings. *Scott Taylor*

The reason for the counterweight was the extremely long T15E2 main gun. This weapon was 5.5 feet longer than the M3 main gun found on the T26E3. *Scott Taylor*

The T26E4's travel lock was a different casting and was considerably taller than the one used on other Pershings. *Scott Taylor*

Despite these differences, the travel lock's purpose was the same as travel locks used on the conventional Pershings. *Scott Taylor*

Inspired by the heavily armored M2A3E2 "Jumbo" medium tank, the Army authorized the development of a similarly up-armored Pershing, the T26E5. This tank had turret armor 8 inches thick on the front, with a gun shield up to 11 inches thick, and thicker armor on the hull. A heavier-duty equilibrator was required to offset the greatly increased weight of the gun shield, and extended "duckbill" track end connectors were installed on the outer sides of the tracks for better flotation. Seen during testing at Aberdeen Proving Ground on August 6, 1945, is the first pilot T26E5, registration number 30150824 and serial number 10007. *Chun Hsu collection*

Stenciled on the sand shield of this vehicle are "HVY. TK. T26E5" and "23" RUB. TR. T84," a reference to the T84 rubber tracks, which were 23 inches wide. The duckbill end connectors added another 5 inches to the width of the track assemblies. *Patton Museum*

The third T26E5, serial number 10009 and registration number 30150826 (with an "S" suffix to indicate that the vehicle's radio shielding has been tested), is seen during evaluations by the Army Ground Forces Board No. 2 Test Operation. This vehicle lacked the duckbill track connectors. The redesigned, thicker gun shield is visible in profile. *Chun Hsu collection*

As a result of the commendable record of 105 mm howitzers mounted in Sherman tanks on the battlefields of the Pacific and Europe, the Army investigated the suitability of installing such a weapon in the T261E1 Pershing tank, using the M4 105 mm howitzer on a T117 combination mount (standardized later as M71). The result was the T26E2 heavy tank. For the production pilot vehicle, the Detroit Tank Arsenal manufactured the chassis, and the Fisher Tank Arsenal built the turret. This pilot, registration number 30131576, was delivered to Aberdeen Proving Ground in July 1945, and it was the subject of this series of photos taken during that month. *Chun Hsu collection*

The pilot T26E2 was photographed at Aberdeen on July 18, 1945, after receiving new markings on the sand shields. Although a dustcover hides the howitzer shield, or mantlet, in these photos, that shield was a different design than that of the T26 90 mm guns, having a thickness of up to 8 inches of armor. The thickness of the front of the turret was increased to 5 inches, compared to 4 inches for the T26E3. *Chun Hsu collection*

A muffler was not a part of the exhaust system of the T26E3/M26, but one was mounted on the rear of the hull of the pilot T26E2 heavy tank. Braces with turnbuckles, for proper tensioning, were provided for the rear mudguards. Two brackets for an engine hoist are present on the left side of the turret, as are a track jack and a section of four spare track shoes. *Chun Hsu collection*

Further details of the muffler are disclosed in this rear view of the pilot T26E2. To the sides and rear of the muffler is what appears to be a brush guard, made of steel plate. The exhaust outlet above the muffler lacks a travel lock. *Chun Hsu collection*

The pilot T26E2 is viewed from above at Aberdeen Proving Ground on July 18, 1945. In addition to the pedestal mount for a .50-caliber machine gun in the usual position on top of the turret bustle, an additional mount for a machine gun, in the form of a socket on a short pedestal with triangular braces, was mounted on a steel plate to the front of the commander's cupola. To the immediate left of that mount was a vane sight, and to the rear of the mount was a device, visible in other photos of the pilot T26E2, that may have been a mount for a sighting device, such as a panoramic telescope. *Chun Hsu collection*

The nickname "LITTLE PETER" is stenciled on the sand shield of this T26E2, registration number 30131576, during testing of the vehicle by Army Ground Forces Board No. 2, at Fort Knox, Kentucky, in an undated photo. The .50-caliber M2 HB machine gun has been stored on the travel position on brackets on the rear of the turret bustle; the barrel of the gun, which normally would be removed from the receiver for travel, is jutting to the rear of the turret. *Chun Hsu collection*

Two turretless Pershing tank chassis are in the foreground of a view of T26E2s undergoing assembly at the Detroit Tank Arsenal. Eleven of the vehicles have turrets installed, and more chassis without turrets are in the background. On the first vehicles with turrets in the lines to the left and the center, an exhaust outlet is present on the rear of the hull, with no muffler; evidently, a muffler was present on the pilot T26E2 only. The travel lock present on the exhaust outlet of the M26 tank was not used on the T26E2, due to the shortness of the howitzer tube. The extra machine-gun mount to the front of the commander's cupola, seen on the pilot T26E2, seems to have been discontinued on production vehicles, although the vane sight remained in place in that area. *FCA North America Archives*

A T26E2 hull is being tested for watertightness in a water tank outside the Detroit Tank Arsenal building, while six other T26E2s are parked to the sides of the tank. A ramp is on each end of the tank, to allow the tanks to drive in and out. Parked in the background next to the building are several tanks, including what appear to be several M26s. *FCA North America Archives*

A T26E2 is parked outside the Detroit Tank Arsenal, with a sign commemorating the presentation of an Army-Navy excellence award to the arsenal on August 10, 1942. The Detroit Tank Arsenal produced a total of 185 of these tanks; production ended in 1945. *Chun Hsu collection*

Dustcovers are over the bow and antiaircraft machine guns on a T26E2, and a machine gun tripod is stored on the right fender. After World War II, these vehicles were standardized as the M45 medium tank. A limited number of them were used in the Korean War. *Patton Museum*

Employees of the Detroit Tank Arsenal pose on the last of the 185 T26E2s to be completed. According to the sign, the tank was built on August 28, 1945; the turret was assembled on September 15, 1945; and the vehicle was shipped on September 26, 1945. Chalked on the forward end of the sand shield are "LAST ONE" along with some numbers. *Patton Museum*

Posing for a group photo on the final T26E2, near the end of September 1945, are executives of the Detroit Tank Arsenal. This was registration number 30131617. The end of World War II spelled the cessation of further production of the Pershing tanks. However, the tank served as the basis or an improved medium tank, the M46, and the Pershings would go on to serve with distinction in the Korean War. *Patton Museum*

The M26A1 medium tank represented existing M26s whose original M3 90 mm gun in the M67 mount was replaced by improved versions of that gun and mount: the M3A1 90 mm gun in the M67A1 mount. The M3A1 was distinguished by its single-baffle muzzle brake and a bore evacuator to the rear of the muzzle brake. The bore evacuator drew propellant fumes forward out of the barrel, away from the interior of the turret. The bore evacuator on the M3A1 90 mm gun on this M26A1, registration number 30127583 S, is a shorter version than those sometimes seen on other M26A1s.

The two pilot M26E1s were produced to test the suitability of the T54 90 mm gun in the Pershing tank. The T54 replicated the ballistic performance of the T15E2 90 mm gun of the T26E4 tank, but with a single-unit projectile and propellant casing and a shorter gun tube. As seen in a photo of the second pilot M26E1, the 90 mm gun was equipped with a single-baffle muzzle brake, effected by removing the front baffle from a standard muzzle brake. This resulted in a frustum shape (i.e., conical, with the tip cut off). Among other internal improvements, a concentric recoil system was installed on the 90 mm gun mount, to take up less space. *Chun Hsu collection*

Like the double-baffle muzzle brake of the M3 90 mm gun of the T26E3/M26, the single-baffle muzzle brake of the M3A1 90 mm gun was designed to direct the muzzle blast of the gun to the sides, to limit the amount of dust stirred up when the gun was fired. Excessive dust could prevent a gunner from accurately firing the gun after the first shot. The muzzle brake also served to reduce the recoil of the gun. M26A1s with the M3A1 90 mm gun saw service in the Korean War.

In 1948, Detroit Tank Arsenal converted an M26 medium tank to a more modern tank, the M26E2 medium tank. The key changes were in the power pack, comprising a Continental AV-1790 twelve-cylinder, air-cooled engine and a cross-drive transmission. The engine was rated at 810 horsepower, significantly higher than the 500-horsepower Ford engine that powered the T26E3/M26. Only one of these vehicles was produced, registration number 3012420, seen during tests at Aberdeen Proving Ground in May 1948. *US Army Armor & Cavalry Collection*

CHAPTER 5
The Pershing in Korea

Sometime after World War II, the M26 was dubbed the "Pershing," honoring General of the Armies John Joseph Pershing, the highest-ranking US officer of all time. While it was the most powerful tank in the US arsenal immediately after World War II, with only 2,212 produced, they were vastly outnumbered by Shermans. Because their size, the Pershings did not lend themselves to service in occupied Japan, and most were assigned to US-based and European units.

When North Korean troops invaded South Korea on June 25, 1950, led by Soviet-produced T-34-85 tanks, the South Koreans had few effective antitank guns, which permitted the North to rapidly advance. The United States, coming to the South's aid, had few tanks in the Pacific, and even fewer of the Pershings. Three derelict M26s were located at the Tokyo Ordnance Depot and were quickly rehabilitated and rushed to Korea, where they joined a handful of M24 Chaffees in forming a provisional tank platoon. The platoon was used in the defense of Chinju on July 28, but the Pershings quickly broke down, the failing being often attributed to the use of incorrect fan belts, which led to the tanks being abandoned.

Since the Shermans were deemed inadequate to counter the T-34-85, efforts were made to rush more of the Pershings into action. The Army sent three battalions. The 70th Tank Battalion, a training unit at Fort Knox, stripped the base of M26s serving as monuments and processed them through the base shops and shipped out for Korea. Another training unit, the 73rd Tank Battalion, based at Fort Benning, also deployed, as did the 89th Tank Battalion, raised from various tank units in the Pacific, deployed with a single company of M26s.

The Marines rearmed a company from the 1st Marine Brigade and dispatched them to Korea.

These Marines were the first of these four units to engage the enemy. On August 17, 1950, four T-34-85s of the North Korean Peoples Army (NKPA) advanced on Pusan. Initially encountering Marines with ineffective bazookas, the Soviet-built tanks continued their advance, and as they came around a hill they encountered a Marine M26. Mistaking the Pershing for the easily defeated Chaffee, they continued their advance unchecked—until the Marines pierced the NKPA tank with two 90 mm rounds, setting off a catastrophic ammunition explosion. The second T-34 also was taken under fire by bazooka-armed Marines, to no effect. Two Marine Pershings placed several 90 mm rounds into that tank as well, blowing it up. The Marine tankers also destroyed the third T-34, causing the commander of the fourth T-34-85 to order his tank into a hasty retreat.

Pershing crewmen of the Army got into the action near Tabu-dong when M26s from Company C, 73rd Tank Battalion, destroyed thirteen T-34-85s and five SU-76M assault guns in the span of two days.

These actions were a foretelling of the future actions between the Pershing and the T-34-85. Around the Pusan perimeter, near Inchon or Kimpo, tank battles were increasingly one sided, with the Pershings readily dispatching the Communist tanks.

The M26s were involved in thirty-eight tank-versus-tank actions in Korea, and six Pershings were knocked out, but many were repaired. The Communists lost at least ninety-seven T-34-85s.

The crew of an M26 medium tank poses with the vehicle in a field at Fort Knox, Kentucky, around 1949. The vehicle is an early-production example, with two periscopes per driver. The front mudguards and the forward sections of the sand shields have been removed. T81 single-pin tracks are installed. *Kevin Emdee collection*

An M45 medium tank (originally, T26E2) is assuming an attack position during a training exercise at Fort Knox, Kentucky, on November 8, 1949. The crew has swabbed mud on the howitzer tube and mantlet, the turret, and stowage boxes for camouflage and has put the rack for the drivers' hoods to use as a storage rack for two 5-gallon liquid containers. *National Archives*

When the Communist Korean People's Army invaded the Republic of Korea on June 25, 1950, the United States and United Nations had to scramble to insert troops and armor on the Korean peninsula. The Communists were equipped with the potent, Soviet-made T-34-85, so a tank to match the firepower and protection of that vehicle, the M26 Pershing, was brought into the theater. Three derelict M26s from the Tokyo Ordnance Depot were repaired and turned over to crews under 1Lt. Samuel R. Fowler. They arrived with the Pershings at Pusan on July 16. One of the three tanks is shown with two M24 Chaffee light tanks and several M8 armored cars in a valley near Taegu on July 22, 1950. The registration number of the M26, except for the last digit, is on the rear storage box: 3012794. *National Archives*

A crewman is checking the .50-caliber M2 HB machine gun on this M26, registration number 30127945, outside Taegu on July 22, 1950. In the background is another one of Lt. Fowler's three M26s.

The gunner of one of Lt. Fowler's three M26s, registration number 30128565, is zeroing in the 90 mm gun at a makeshift range outside Taegu on July 22, 1950. Subsequently, the three tanks and their crews were transported to Chinju, where that force conducted a last-stand battle with Communist forces on July 31. All three tanks and eight of the crewmen were lost in the fighting. *National Archives*

This Pershing is one of the first three tanks rebuilt in Japan and rushed to Korea in July 1950. Only semigloss Olive Drab paint and basic markings were applied. These three dispatched Pershings overheated because they had the wrong fan belts.

Despite "ALICE's" appearance in August 27, 1950, the M26, for the most part, was in its as-built configuration. The tank even retains its World War II–era Blue Drab registration number (U.S.A. 30127281) and sand shields.

Two members of Company A, 1st Tank Battalion, 1st Marine Division, at San Diego, California, are preparing an M26 prior to embarking for Korea in early July 1950. The USMC registration number, 118011, is stenciled to the lower right of the exhaust outlet. The tank in the right background has a US Army registration number, which is not fully legible. *National Archives*

M26 medium tanks played a key role in the defense of the Pusan Perimeter, as North Korean forces pressed southward in the summer of 1950. The 1st Marine Tank Battalion, equipped with Pershing tanks, landed at Pusan on August 2 as part of the 1st Provisional Marine Brigade. The following day, this series of photos was taken as M26s of that battalion were embarked on railroad flatcars for shipment to the front. A partial USMC registration number, "1180," with the last two digits hidden, is to the lower right of the exhaust outlet of the closest Pershing. *National Archives*

Members of the 1st Marine Tank Battalion at Pusan Harbor are preparing to move to the fighting front on August 3, 1950. The closest M26 and the one in the preceding photo were equipped with T81 single-pin tracks. Packing tubes with 90 mm ammunition are secured to the flatcar in the foreground. Seventeen M26s, one M4A3(105) with a dozer blade, and one M32B3 recovery vehicle were loaded on flatcars at Pusan. *National Archives*

Wooden crates are tied with ropes to the engine deck of an M26 medium tank on a flatcar at Pusan. On the rear of the turret bustle is stored a .50-caliber M2 HB machine gun with a dustcover installed over it. The 5-gallon liquid container on the rear of the right fender is stenciled "OE-30," for the class of motor oil it contained. *National Archives*

At Pusan, the Marine to the right is checking the call box on the rear of the hull of an M26. The tow pintle of the tank is stowed to the lower left of the exhaust outlet. The number 15 is painted on the dustcover of the .50-caliber machine gun, above the loader's hatch. *National Archives*

Members of the 1st Marine Tank Battalion are loading 90 mm ammunition into the loader's hatch of an M26 at Pusan Harbor. Such was the haste of the battalion to jump into combat as soon it arrived at the front lines that gunners of the M26s zeroed in their gunsights by firing at targets while still loaded on the flatcars at their destination, Changwon. *National Archives*

During the battle for the Pusan Perimeter, troops from the 1st Cavalry Division are assembled near an M26 to receive a tutorial on the tank on August 10, 1950. Three days earlier, Company B, 70th Tank Battalion, had arrived at Pusan with M26 tanks; that company would provide armored support to the 8th Cavalry Regiment, of the 1st Cavalry Division. Markings for the twenty-fifth vehicle of Company B, 70th Tank Battalion, are present on the bow of the tank. *National Archives*

An M26 medium tank is dueling with Communist forces on a distant hilltop on a road to Sach-on, in the Masan-Chinju area of Korea on August 10, 1950. The tracks are the T81s. A rolled tarpaulin is strapped to the right side of the vehicle, and bedrolls, an entrenching tool, and other gear are hanging from the turret. *National Archives*

On August 15, 1950, a Pershing from Company A, 1st Marine Tank Battalion, has paused on a road through a pass in a ridgeline west of Yongsan while supporting troops of the 1st Cavalry Division. The rear of the left fender and sand shield are crumpled. The pistol port on the turret is open, and the .50-caliber M2 HB machine gun barrel is secured in its rest. *US Army Armor & Cavalry Collection*

An M26 from Company A, 1st Marine Tank Battalion, numbered "34" on the side of the turret, has paused in the same pass shown in the preceding photo, turret trained to the left, while infantrymen take a break to the front of the tank. Commanding this tank was TSgt. Cecil Fullerton. *US Army Armor & Cavalry Collection*

In a third photo taken at the same pass west of Yongsan, a bit farther down the road from the site of the preceding photo, a Pershing with a number "2" on the turret (the full number appears to have been "32") has its turret trained to the left on August 17, 1950. Spent 90 mm shell casings are in the foreground. Later on in the evening of that date, during the First Battle of Naktong Bulge, Company A, 1st Marine Tank Battalion, fought in the first engagement between M26s and North Korean T-34-85s in this vicinity, destroying three enemy tanks. *US Army Armor & Cavalry Collection*

The crewmen of an M26 medium tank in a static position have heavily camouflaged the vehicle with tree branches during operations in August 1950. A crewman is standing in the cupola hatch, another is manning the .50-caliber machine gun, and a third one is crouched on the side of the turret, binoculars at the ready. *National Archives*

Very faintly visible on the ventilator bulge on the top of the glacis of this M26, crossing a bridge in the Taegu-Waegwan sector on August 20, 1950, is the nickname "DOROTHY." The tank was serving with Company C, 73rd Tank Battalion. Beginning on August 18 and continuing through the 24th, Pershings of this company fought off nightly attacks by the enemy, including assaults by T-34-85s, in a zone nicknamed the "Bowling Alley." *National Archives*

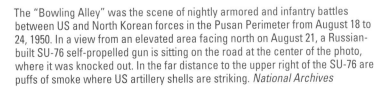

The "Bowling Alley" was the scene of nightly armored and infantry battles between US and North Korean forces in the Pusan Perimeter from August 18 to 24, 1950. In a view from an elevated area facing north on August 21, a Russian-built SU-76 self-propelled gun is sitting on the road at the center of the photo, where it was knocked out. In the far distance to the upper right of the SU-76 are puffs of smoke where US artillery shells are striking. *National Archives*

This Pershing was assigned to Company C, 73rd Tank Battalion. It appeared in position in the "Bowling Alley" near Tabu-dong on August 24, 1950. Tabu-dong had some of the fiercest tank action in the Korean War. The tank battles took place in seven consecutive nightly clashes between US and North Korean armor.

Two M26s from Company B, 89th Tank Battalion, have been emplaced on earth ramps to be used as howitzers to support the operations of the 29th Infantry Regiment along the Pusan Perimeter on August 25, 1950. Deploying the tanks in this manner allowed the 90 mm guns to achieve the elevation necessary to conduct indirect-fire missions against enemy positions. The registration number of the closest tank is visible on the center storage box: 30127817. *National Archives*

A crewman crouching on a storage box on the right side of a US Army M26 is scanning through binoculars for targets near Tabu-dong on August 24, 1950. Next to that GI, boxes for .30-caliber machine gun ammunition have been stashed in the rack intended for storing drivers' hoods. *US Army Armor & Cavalry Collection*

In another photo taken in the Tabu-dong area on August 24, 1950, an M26 is rolling down a road next to a hut, taking a detour around the destroyed bridge in the right foreground. Two nicknames are painted on this tank: an illegible one on the top center of the glacis, and "PATSY-ANN" on the side of the front storage box on the left fender. *US Army Armor & Cavalry Collection*

An M26 medium tank is maneuvering past a T-34-85 knocked out along the ad through the "Bowling Alley," on August 24, 1950. The enemy tank is marked with graffiti: "27TH INF." and "COURTESY FOX CO." On the rears of the fenders of the M26 are markings for the eleventh vehicle of Company C, 73rd Tank Battalion, which was prominent in the battle of the "Bowling Alley," and the nickname "PAT" is painted on the side of the front storage box on the fender. Painting women's names—presumably of wives and girlfriends—on the tanks was a practice of this tank battalion. Tied above the engine deck is an air-recognition panel, a visual to help friendly pilots avoid attacking the tank. Exhaust air from the radiator fans would cause these panels to billow like this. *US Army Armor & Cavalry Collection*

The same Pershing shown in the preceding photo, number 11 from Company C, 73rd Tank Battalion, is parked among the same assortment of knocked-out T-34-85 tanks on August 24, 1950. Here, the recognition panel is crumpled up on the engine deck. *US Army Armor & Cavalry Collection*

An M26 is advancing on the road through the Bowling Alley on August 24, 1950, with two knocked-out T-34-85s in the left foreground and background. When the photo was taken, the crew of the Pershing was firing at a party of North Koreans placing mines in the distance. On the road ahead of the M26 is a knocked-out North Korean SU-76 self-propelled gun. *US Army Armor & Cavalry Collection*

The "PAT" inscription on the storage box is clearer in this photo of the crew replenishing the vehicle's stores of 90 mm ammunition during a pause in the action along the Bowling Alley. Fiberboard packing tubes for the ammunition are lying on the ground in the foreground, and an M1 carbine is resting on the air-recognition panel on the engine deck. Two knocked-out T-34-85s are in the background. *US Army Armor & Cavalry Collection*

"MARGARET #2" is the nickname painted on the ventilator bulge of vehicle number 13 of Company C, 73rd Tank Battalion, photographed on August 27, 1950. The nickname "MARGARET #2" also is repeated on the side of the front left storage box. The names of the drivers are painted to the fronts of their hatches: only "CPL" is visible for the driver, but the assistant driver is "PVT GLENN." *US Army Armor & Cavalry Collection*

An M26 nicknamed "ALICE" is moving onto a road in the Pusan Perimeter on August 27, 1950. The registration number, 30127281, is faintly visible below the nickname on the ventilator bulge. Coming up behind is an M26 bearing the nickname "MARGARET." *US Army Armor & Cavalry Collection*

With its air-recognition panel billowing from the airflow from the radiator fans, an M26 from the 73rd Tank Battalion is proceeding along a road on August 27, 1950. Field packs, boots, canteens, and an air-recognition flag are secured to the turret bustle, and several boxes are stuffed into the rack for the drivers' hoods. *US Army Armor & Cavalry Collection*

An M26 medium tank from Company C, 72nd Tank Battalion, is shelling North Korean positions in the Naktong Bulge on August 31, 1950. The tank is furnished with T84E1 tracks, a double-pin, rubber-tread type with chevron grousers. Partly hidden to the rear of the tank is an M19 40 mm Multiple Gun Motor Carriage, with two 40 mm automatic guns, which appears to be participating in the shelling. *US Army Armor & Cavalry Collection*

Near the Naktong River around late August or early September 1950, four US Army M26s are firing at an enemy observation post across the river. All four tanks have air-recognition panels on the tops of their turret bustles. The vehicle commanders are not wearing head protection. On the closest Pershing, two 5-gallon liquid containers are on the forward part of the right fender, while another liquid container is in the drivers' hood rack on the turret. *US Army Armor & Cavalry Collection*

M26 tanks are lined up in a field during the latter part of the fighting in the Naktong Bulge, on September 2, 1950. On the closest tank, the door of the forward storage box on the left fender is open, and ammunition boxes are stowed on the fender, with a simple rack made of steel rods to hold them in place. A "3" representing the vehicle number is on the turret to the front of the pistol port; equipment hides the platoon number preceding the vehicle number. *National Archives*

Near Yongsan on September 3, 1950, a GI, *left*, is motioning the driver of an M26 into a defensive position during the September 1–5 battle for that village, part of the defense of the Pusan Perimeter. On the fender of the M26 is a simple rack, evidently made of steel rods, to allow the crew to stow more equipment on the fender. In the background are supply trucks, another M26, and an M4A3E8 medium tank. *National Archives*

A USMC M26 medium tank numbered "34" on the turret has struck a land mine, blowing the right track apart, during fighting near Myong-Ni. This occurred at about the same time the crew spotted an approaching enemy tank. Crouching to the left are two infantrymen. This vehicle has a storage rack on the fender, formed of steel strips. Ammunition boxes are crowded into the rack. *National Archives*

Doughs of the 9th Infantry Regiment, 2nd Infantry Division, are hitching a ride on an M26 medium tank during a counterattack across the Naktong River on September 3, 1950. This was during the Second Battle of Naktong Bulge, which lasted from September 1 to 15. The left mudguard is missing from the front of the fender. The bulge finally was secured in mid-September 1950, when the US X Corps landings at Inchon caused the North Koreans to abandon the Pusan Perimeter. *US Army Armor & Cavalry Collection*

Two M26s with markings for Company A, 73rd Tank Battalion, are parked next to a Sherman tank with vertical-volute suspension system at Pusan on September 10, 1950, while waiting to board transports for the Inchon landings. Crewmen have hung their clothing out to dry on a line rigged between the two Pershings. As a modification, the M26 on the right has cylinders over the apertures for the gunner's sight and the coaxial machine gun. *US Army Armor & Cavalry Collection*

Members of the crew of an M26 marked for vehicle 12, Company C, 73rd Tank Battalion, and registration number 30127281, are taking a cigarette break while awaiting shipment from the port of Pusan in September 1950. On the right upper rear of the hull is an infantry call box, with a metal conduit routed from its bottom to the hull below the right taillight. *US Army Armor & Cavalry Collection*

After the Inchon landings of September 15, 1950, the Communists' main supply route into the south quickly was cut off, and the UN forces took advantage of this to mount an offensive to break out of the Pusan Perimeter on September 15. Here, an M26 from Company B, 70th Tank Battalion, is advancing through a settlement near Taegu, en route to Waegwan, during the breakout on September 17. In addition to the .50-caliber machine gun mounted above the turret bustle, a .30-caliber machine gun with a conical flash suppressor on the muzzle is on a short pedestal mount to the front of the commander's cupola. *National Archives*

A rare image of an M45 medium tank in the Korean War shows registration number 30131581 fording the Kumho River during the breakout from the Pusan Perimeter on September 18, 1950. The tank was assigned to the 6th Tank Battalion. The round object on the side of the turret below the muzzle of the .50-caliber machine gun is the open door of the pistol port. *US Army Armor & Cavalry Collection*

An emplaced M26 medium tank has been heavily camouflaged with bunches of tall grass. A shirt is hanging from the bow machine gun, and a webbing belt with a pistol in a holster is hanging above the small chair under the bow. The tracks are the two-pin T84E1 type, rubber shoes with chevron grousers. A .30-caliber machine gun is mounted to the front of the commander's cupola, to supplement the .50-caliber machine gun mounted on the turret bustle. *US Army Armor & Cavalry Collection*

M45 medium tanks of the 6th Tank Battalion are fording the Kumho River during the breakout from the Pusan Perimeter, likely on September 18, 1950. On the lead tank, with the dustcover for the 105 mm howitzer mount removed, the travel lock at the bottom center of the shield, or mantlet, is visible. *National Archives*

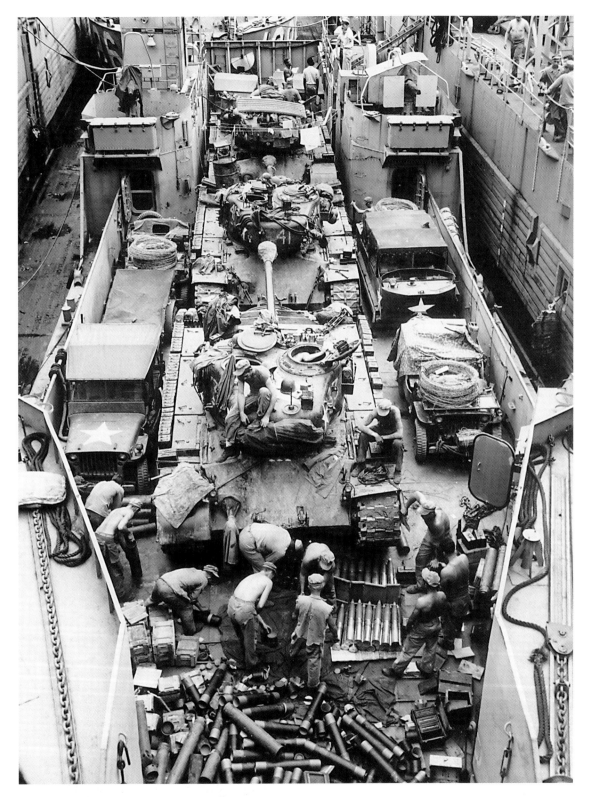

Pershing tanks from the 1st Marine Tank Battalion are sharing the deck of a landing craft with several jeeps and an M29 Weasel in preparation for the landings at Inchon in September 1950. In the foreground, Marines are preparing 90 mm ammunition. The nearest M26 is number 3 from the 3rd Platoon, Company A, 1st Marine Tank Battalion. This was a veteran of the battle with the North Korean T-34-85s in the Pusan Perimeter in August, and kill markings for three T-34s are painted on the ventilator bulge at the top of the glacis. This photo gives a good idea of how ammunition boxes were stowed in the racks on the outer parts of the fenders. *National Archives*

While Pershings were seeing combat in Korea, other M26s were employed in occupation duty in Europe. This example is participating in Exercise Rainbow, a joint US Army, Air Force, and Navy readiness exercise in the Federal Republic of Germany from September 11 to 18, 1950. *National Archives*

During the breakout from the Pusan Perimeter in September 1950, an M26 medium tank has taken position across a roadway in the Tabu-dong area, north of Taegu, while infantrymen take a break. The Pershing has very little baggage and equipment stored on its exterior, with the exception of a 5-gallon liquid container stashed in the rack for the drivers' hoods. *National Archives*

Communist forces captured the city of Seoul three days after storming south of the 38th parallel in late June 1950. In September of that year, United Nations forces liberated the city after a week of bitter street fighting. Here, an M26 from the 1st Marine Division, hatches buttoned up, provides support to infantrymen as they scramble past a burning building in Seoul on September 27, 1950. *National Museum of the United States Marine Corps*

A USMC M26 marked "B11" on the turret, for first tank, 1st Platoon, Company B, has taken up a position on a street during the Second Battle of Seoul, in late September 1950. Ammo boxes are lined up on the fender, held in place with webbing straps. A water can is jammed into the rack for the drivers' hoods on the turret. A tank crewman's helmet is resting on the pedestal on the top of the turret bustle. As a mark of the Communist occupation of Seoul, portraits of Josef Stalin and Kim Il-sung, premier of North Korea, are on the building in the background. *National Archives*

This M26 was assigned to the 72nd Tank Battalion and supported the 9th Infantry Regiment along the Naktong River in September 1950. Although the Pershing saw only limited use in World War II, it proved itself in Korea.

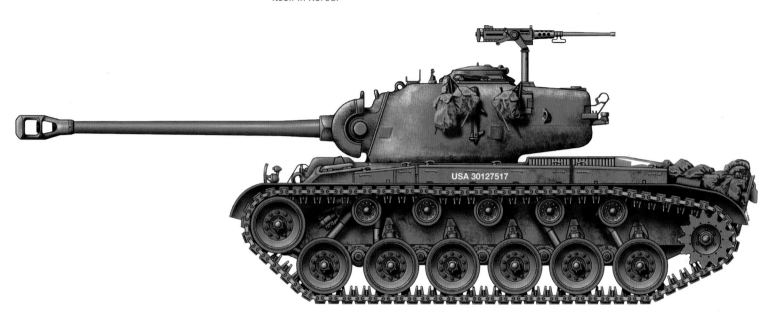

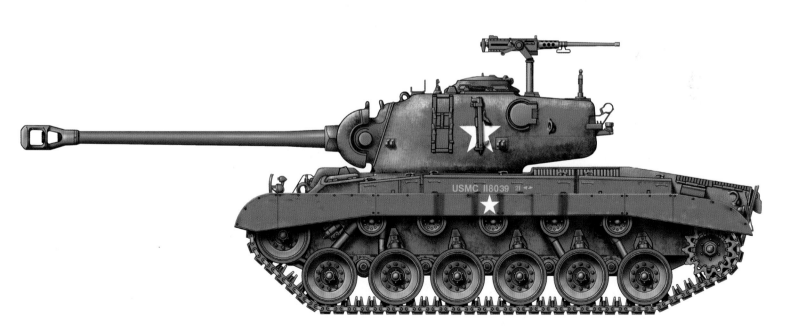

Tanks of 1st Platoon, Company B, 1st Marine Tank Battalion, were key to the fighting near Kimpo airbase in September 1950. Most USMC Pershings did not display the national symbol (star), but this one is an exception to that rule.

An M26 from the 1st Marine Division detonated a mine near Hongcheon, Korea, which destroyed the right track and the front of the suspension and created a crater under the tank. To the rear, another M26 has come to a stop. A dozen spent 90 mm shell casings are lying on the ground to the left. Two M1 carbines are leaning against the glacis to the right. *National Archives*

Infantrymen of the 1st Marine Division infantrymen are taking cover behind an M26 marked as the fifth vehicle of the 2nd Platoon of Company B, while they are firing at Communist troops to the right. Another M26 is in view in the left background. *National Archives*

In the fall of 1950, United Nations forces drove far into North Korea, but then the military intervention of China in the Korean conflict reversed that tide, from November 27 to December 13 encircling the 1st Marine Division in the area of the Chosin Reservoir. During that bitter fighting on December 6, a photographer recorded this view and the next one of M26A1 medium tanks of the 1st Marine Division with infantrymen after successfully thwarting an enemy ambush. *National Archives*

The same M26A1 in the preceding photo, along with another one behind it, are leading a vehicular column, turrets turned to the left. The guns are the characteristic M3A1 90 mm gun, with single-baffle muzzle brakes and bore evacuators to the rears of the brakes. *National Archives*

Marine Corps M26s of 2nd Platoon, Company A, 1st Tank Battalion, are in position, guarding a supply route at Majon-dong, about 20 miles south of the Chosin Reservoir, on December 9, 1950. The route led north from there to Koto-ri and then Chosin. A third M26 is in the background to the far right. All three tanks have .50-caliber M2 HB machine guns on pedestal mounts to the fronts of the commanders' cupolas. *National Archives*

A crewman is standing next to M26 number 1 of the 2nd Platoon, Company A, 1st Tank Battalion, at Majon-dong on December 9, 1951. Two helmets with camouflage covers are hanging from the turret, and boxes for .50-caliber and .30-caliber ammunition are stored on the fender. This position commanded the main supply road along which the 1st Marine Division was retreating from the Chosin Reservoir. *National Archives*

On December 13, 1950, a tank from Company B, 1st Tank Battalion, 1st Marine Division, is boarding LCT-675 at Hungnam, North Korea, during the evacuation of US and United Nations forces following the Battle of the Chosin Reservoir. The tank is banking onto the LCT's ramp, with its turret traversed to the rear. A large amount of baggage, field packs, and even a broom are stowed on the vehicle. *National Archives*

An M26 of the Marine Corps' 1st Tank Battalion is guarding a roadblock a short distance west of the 1st Marine Division's command post at Masan, a coastal town west of Pusan, Korea, on December 24, 1950. A bin that appears to be of sheet metal holds eleven .30-caliber ammunition boxes on the fender. On the side of the turret, the number "34," signifying 3rd Platoon, fourth vehicle, is visible. *National Archives*

On March 2, 1951, a 1st Marine Division M26 medium tank is maneuvering through the wreckage of trucks of a US Army unit ambushed two weeks before during the Battle of Hoengsong, in South Korea. The gun mount lacks a dustcover, but what appear to be both drivers' hoods are present in the rack on the side of the turret. Two 5-gallon liquid containers, over a dozen ammo boxes, and a field pack or bag are on the fender, held by a steel-rod rack. *National Archives*

"USMC" is marked on the ventilator bulge, and "D11," signifying first vehicle, 1st Platoon, Company D, is on the turret and the glacis of an M26 crossing a bridge during a march to Wonju, in South Korea, during February 1951. An oil drum is lashed to the engine deck. Another M26 is coming up to the rear. *National Archives*

After an all-night road march in the rain, the crews of a number of M26s, M4A3E8s, and vehicles of the 1st Marine Tank Battalion have encamped south of Chungju, in South Korea, prior to closing with the enemy on the central front, on February 22, 1951. In the foreground, the second M26 from the left is marked "C-25" on the turret. *National Archives*

At the same bivouac area seen in the preceding photo, crewmen from the number 1 vehicle from 2nd Platoon, Company C, 1st Marine Tank Battalion, are cleaning mud from the front of their M26 medium tank on February 22, 1951. A metal can, an M1 helmet, and two canteens are hanging on the rear of the turret bustle, and another canteen is hanging by the retainer chain for its cap from an antenna atop the bustle. *National Archives*

An M26 of the 1st Marine Tank Battalion is carefully navigating across a stream outside Hoengsong on March 8, 1951. Retreating Chinese Communist forces had heavily mined the area, including with a large number of improvised explosive devices. *National Archives*

These 1st Marine Division tanks and infantry are moving forward on the central front in Korea around March 1951. The tanks are M26s, with the exception of the third vehicle, an M4A3(105) HVSS. Markings on the turrets are for Company C, 1st Tank Battalion. *National Archives*

Infantrymen from the 1st Marine Division are firing at enemy troops from the shelter of an M26 medium tank, on the central front in Korea in March 1951. The front mudguards have been removed from the fenders, and a tow chain is wrapped around the tow eyes on the bottom of the glacis. Another tank is on the road in the background. *National Archives*

These 1st Marine Division infantrymen have dismounted from Pershing tanks they have been riding on and are marching forward to Hongcheon in March 1951. Similar to those on the tank in the preceding photo, the mudguards are missing from the M26 in the background. *National Archives*

A mine has blown the right track off a Marine Corps M26 medium tank outside Hongcheon on March 30, 1951. The tank was from 3rd Platoon, Company C, 1st Marine Tank Battalion, as signified by the "C-32" marking on the bow. Another M26 and several other vehicles are approaching over the crest of the hill in the background. *National Archives*

An M26 medium tank is approaching a shot-up cargo truck in Korea in April 1951. There are three faint, light-colored markings on the ventilator bulge that resemble the T-34-85 kill markings, previously shown, on the M26 marked "A-33," from 3rd Platoon, Company A, 1st Marine Tank Battalion.

Marines are awaiting a recovery vehicle for an M26 severely damaged when it detonated two enemy mines outside Hwacheon between April 22 and 26, 1951. The tank was "C-12," from 1st Platoon, Company C, 1st Marine Tank Battalion. The blasts tore the idler and the sprocket from the hull and flung the two front bogie-wheel assemblies clear of the tank. Machine-gun ammo boxes are piled up on the right rear of the engine deck. *National Archives*

In another photo taken near Hwacheon around April 22–26, 1951, M26 "C-11" from 1st Platoon, Company, C 1st Marine Tank Brigade, is mired on a dirt road near a hilltop. "USMC" is stenciled over the identification star on the glacis. On a stake driven into the ground to the rear of the crewman standing in the loader's hatch is a human skull. *National Archives*

At a site identified as "New Yanggu, N. Korea," M26 medium tank "B-21" sits in a valley, its right track and suspension damaged by a Chinese mine, in June 1951. The rubber tire has been ripped off the rear-outboard bogie wheel, and the rear of the right fender has been blown off. *National Archives*

Marines are preparing to hook up a boom cable from an M32A1B3 tank recovery vehicle to the front end of a mine-damaged M26 medium tank, "B-22," registration number 30128393, near Yanggu on June 12, 1951. Lying on the sandy ground are two bogie wheels, a bogie arm, and other suspension parts. In the background is M26 "B41." *National Archives*

An M32A1 tank recovery vehicle, its rear end bucking up into the air, is attempting to lift the front end of a mine-damaged M26 marked A-11, from the 1st Marine Division. The problem was, the crater from the mine explosion was deep, and the Pershing was tightly wedged into the crater, so that instead of lifting the tank with relative ease, the force of the boom cable against the intransigent tank caused the recovery vehicle to rear up. The scene was in the eastern sector of the central front in Korea on June 13, 1951. *National Archives*

An M26 from Company B, 1st Tank Battalion, 1st Marine Division, is blasting away at a Communist bunker north of Won-ni on September 26, 1951. The pistol port on the turret is open, so the loader can eject spent 90 mm casings, a number of which are piled up on the fender storage boxes and the ground alongside the tank. In the foreground are packing tubes for 90 mm ammunition. *National Archives*

At a command post area behind the front lines in Korea, Marines of the 1st Tank Battalion are replenishing the 90 mm ammunition of an M26 medium tank on October 9, 1951. The turret is marked for 1st Platoon, Company D. Pioneer tools, including a sledgehammer and a shovel, are stored on the glacis. In the background is an M26 marked "D-11" on the turret. *National Archives*

At the same time Pershing tanks were fighting Communist forces during the autumn 1951 offensive in Korea, M26s were serving with US and NATO forces in Europe. This M26 from Company C, 63rd Tank Battalion, is crossing a treadway bridge over the Main River near Aschaffenburg, Federal Republic of Germany, in October 1951. In Germany, as in Korea, M26 crews liked to use the rack for the drivers' hoods to store 5-gallon liquid containers. *National Archives*

Members of the 29th Heavy Tank Battalion are preparing their M26s for a battalion exercise at the unit's very muddy motor pool at Kaiserlautern, Federal Republic of Germany, on November 28, 1951. To the lower right, some details of a rack for storing spare track links horizontally are in view. In the center background is the boom of a tank recovery vehicle. *National Archives*

At the firing range at Belsen, Federal Republic of Germany, M26 crews from Company A, 66th Medium Tank Battalion, are preparing to begin a firing exercise on December 11, 1951. On the closer M26, the nickname "AUSTIN" is on the side of the front storage box on the fender, and on the next box to the rear is the registration number, 30128430. In the Army, tank nicknames generally started with the same letter as the company letter. *National Archives*

Infantrymen with M1 Garand rifles and another one behind the .50-caliber machine gun are training their weapons forward during an exercise with an M26 outside Mainz, Federal Republic of Germany, in February 1952. The tank was from Company D, 66th Tank Battalion, and the nickname "DELIRIOUS" is stenciled on the side of the forward storage box. A can of OE-10 motor oil is on the fender. *National Archives*

An M26 nicknamed "DRACULA" is operating with a portable radio crew from the 42nd Armored Infantry Battalion during a field problem near Mainz on February 19, 1952. The tank's unit is not specified but probably was Company D, 66th Tank Battalion. In this photo and the preceding one, the drivers' hoods are stored on their racks on the right side of the turrets. *National Archives*

"DRACULA" is serving as a battle taxi for armored infantrymen during the field problem near Mainz. The identity of the wedge-shaped objects on the fronts of the fenders is unclear; it is possible they were chocks. The spare bogie wheel on the glacis, also seen in the preceding photo, was secured in place with wires. *National Archives*

During the postwar era, the United States supplied some M26 medium tanks to several Allied countries, notably France, Italy, and Belgium. These M26s in the service of the French army are proceeding along a road outside Rastatt in the French occupation zone of the Federal Republic of Germany in spring 1953. *National Archives*

Gen. Alfred M. Gruenther, US Army, Supreme Allied Commander Europe, directly below the soldier standing atop the M26A1, is inspecting a pontoon bridge with officers of French I Corps at the École des Ponts (School for Engineers) in the French occupation zone at Koblenz, Federal Republic of Germany, on August 3, 1953. The rear of the M26A1 is in the foreground, with the turret in the travel position, traversed to the rear. The single-baffle muzzle brake and part of the bore evacuator that distinguished the M26A1 are in view. Also visible are the three pockets, on the top of the dustcover, that enclose the lifting eyes on the gun mount. *National Archives*